Classroom
Strategies
for Helping
At-Risk Students

David R. Snow

with Zoe A. Barley , Patricia A. Lauer,

Sheila A. Arens, Helen S. Apthorp,

Kerry S. Englert, Motoko Akiba

ASCD®

Association for Supervision and Curriculum Development
Alexandria, Virginia USA

McREL

Mid-continent Research for Education and Learning
Aurora, Colorado USA

Association for Supervision and Curriculum Development
1703 N. Beauregard Street • Alexandria, VA 22311-1714 USA
Telephone: 800-933-2723 or 703-578-9600 • Fax: 703-575-5400
Web site: http://www.ascd.org • E-mail: member@ascd.org
Author guidelines: www.ascd.org/write

Mid-continent Research for Education and Learning
2550 S. Parker Road, Suite 500 • Aurora, CO 80014-1678 USA
Telephone: 303-337-0990 • Fax: 303-337-3005
Web site: http://www.mcrel.org • E-mail: info@mcrel.org

Gene R. Carter, *Executive Director;* Nancy Modrak, *Director of Publishing;* Julie Houtz, *Director of Book Editing & Production;* Tim Sniffin, *Project Manager;* Chris Duncan, *Senior Graphic Designer;* Circle Graphics, *Typesetter;* Tracey A. Franklin, *Production Manager*

All Web links in this book are correct as of the publication date below but may have become inactive or otherwise modified since that time. If you notice a deactivated or changed link, please e-mail books@ascd.org with the words "Link Update" in the subject line. In your message, please specify the Web link, the book title, and the page number on which the link appears.

This publication is based on work sponsored wholly, or in part, by the Institute of Education Sciences, U.S. Department of Education, under Contract No. ED-01-CO-0006. The content of this publication does not necessarily reflect the views of IES, the department, or any other agency of the U.S. government.

ASCD publications present a variety of viewpoints. The views expressed or implied in this book should not be interpreted as official positions of the Association.

Paperback ISBN: 1-4166-0202-X • ASCD product #105106 • List Price: $19.95 ($15.95 ASCD member price, direct from ASCD only) s3/05

e-books ($19.95): retail PDF ISBN: 1-4166-0205-4 • netLibrary ISBN 1-4166-0203-8 • ebrary ISBN 1-4166-0204-6

Quantity discounts for the paperback book: 10–49 copies, 10%; 50+ copies, 15%; for 500 or more copies, call 800-933-2723, ext. 5634, or 703-575-5634.

Library of Congress Cataloging-in-Publication Data

Snow, David, 1961-
  Classroom strategies for helping at-risk students / David Snow.
    p. cm.
  Includes bibliographical references and index.
  ISBN 1-4166-0202-X (alk. paper) — ISBN 1-4166-0203-8 (netLibrary) — ISBN 1-4166-0204-6 (ebrary)
  1. Underachievers—Education (Elementary)—United States. 2. Education—Standards—United States. 3. Remedial teaching—United States. I. Mid-continent Research for Education and Learning (Organization) II. Title.

  LC4691.S59 2005
  371.93—dc22
                                                                                          2004028823

12 11 10 09 08 07 06 05   12 11 10 9 8 7 6 5 4 3 2 1

Classroom
Strategies
for Helping
At-Risk Students

Preface	v
Introduction	1
1 Whole-Class Instruction	7
2 Cognitively Oriented Instruction	21
3 Small Groups	33
4 Tutoring	45
5 Peer Tutoring	57
6 Computer-Assisted Instruction	69
Discussion Guide	79
A Final Note to Practitioners	95
Index	97
About the Authors	109

Preface

Mid-continent Research for Education and Learning (McREL), located in Aurora, Colorado, is a private, nonprofit organization founded in 1966. McREL's mission is to make a difference in the quality of education through applied research, product development, and service.

This publication was created based on work completed through McREL's contract with the U.S. Department of Education's Institute of Education Sciences to serve as the regional educational laboratory for the states of Colorado, Kansas, Missouri, Nebraska, North Dakota, South Dakota, and Wyoming. As a regional laboratory, McREL provides field-based research, technical assistance, professional development, evaluation and policy studies, and information services to state and local education agencies in these states.

For more than a decade, McREL has been at the forefront of research, practice, and evaluation related to standards-based education. McREL's national leadership area under the regional laboratory contract is standards-based classroom instruction. This publication, written for practitioners and policymakers, is based on McREL's 2002 research synthesis, *Helping At-Risk Students Meet Standards: A Synthesis of Evidence-Based Classroom Practices*. This publication represents part of McREL's continuing efforts to build on its expertise and research activities, turn reseach into practical guidance, and work with schools, districts, and states to improve their practices and capitalize on the great potential that standards-based education holds for students.

The authors wish to acknowledge the contributions of a number of individuals in the preparation of this publication. Appreciation is extended to external reviewers David Flowers, Marcia Bush Haskin, and Lin Kuzmich, and to McREL staff members Greg Cameron, Zoe Barley, Lou Cicchinelli, Kirsten Miller, Mya Martin-Glenn, Becky Van Buhler, Terry Young, and Robyn Alsop. A debt of gratitude is also owed to the authors of the research that supports this publication. Last but certainly not least, special thanks to Barbara Gaddy for her work on this project. The quality and conceptual design of this publication are largely the result of her work.

This publication, like the McREL synthesis upon which it is based, presents the combined research on programs that provide data specific to the performance of at-risk and low-performing students. The authors recognize the important work of others who have studied interventions and resulting student achievement, but emphasize that the studies presented here were only considered if the results were specifically tied to students deemed to be at risk for failing. It is hoped that principals, curriculum directors, and other readers find the guidance provided in this publication useful in helping low-performing and at-risk students in their schools.

Introduction

S chools and districts across the country long have been focused on ensuring that students succeed in life and participate effectively in society. With the passage of the No Child Left Behind Act, efforts to realize this goal for all students have intensified. Though many children are successfully meeting state and local academic standards, others are not. To improve learning for all students, teachers and school leaders need information and guidance about evidence-based strategies that can assist students who are not meeting standards.

In the summer and fall of 2002, McREL conducted a synthesis of recent research on strategies to assist students during the school day who are low-achieving or at risk of failure (Barley et al., 2002). The resulting work was based on an extensive search and review of published and unpublished studies and qualitative as well as quantitative research. Given the parameters of the literature search and study goals, 118 research studies published between 1985 and 2002 were identified and synthesized. The research team approached the task from a teacher's perspective and asked themselves, "What are effective strategies that can be used in classrooms to assist low-achieving students?" A set of answers to this question lies in the following pages. From this synthesis of research, McREL identified six general classroom strategies, which are reviewed in a condensed form in this book.

Along with a description of each of the strategies, the chapters also report the combined results—a synthesis—of the available research. It is important to stress that this research is limited to studies that isolate program effects for low-performing students. In each case, these results lead to practices that are proven to be effective or at least show promise as effective interventions for at-risk students.

Chapters

This book is composed of the following chapters:

• *Whole-Class Instruction:* McREL defines whole-class instruction as an intervention that involves the teacher working with the entire class simultaneously. Most would think of this as traditional classroom instruction.

• *Cognitively Oriented Instruction:* This chapter analyzes research on cognitive and metacognitive instructional approaches. Effective cognitive strategies leave students thinking about how they learn, and effective metacognitive strategies help students to better plan and reflect. In each case, the students are using skills that are both specifically and generally applicable.

• *Small Groups:* There is significant research on small-group instruction including both like-ability and mixed-ability approaches. This chapter also synthesizes cooperative learning research.

• *Tutoring:* The research on tutoring reveals a wide variety of different types of individuals who tutor at-risk students effectively. The analysis in this chapter includes professional, volunteer, and student tutors.

• *Peer Tutoring:* Peer tutoring is an intervention that pairs students with one another in the classroom. This hybrid of small grouping and tutoring is unique in its approaches and supported by three significant strands of research.

• *Computer-Assisted Instruction:* More and more students are spending time working on computers while they are in school. This chapter reveals the effects that this time can have on student learning.

Terminology

Several terms used throughout this publication are worth defining here:

• *At risk* and *low performing:* In many cases these terms can be, and are, used interchangeably. The only exception here is that very young children may be identified to be *at risk* of falling below standards even before they have been deemed to be *low performing*.
• *Treatment group:* In research, the treatment group is the group being exposed to the intervention. In high quality studies the results of the treatment group are compared with the results of a similar group that did not receive treatment in order to estimate the effect of the treatment (or intervention).

• *Quasi-experimental:* Quasi-experimental designs are characterized by pre- and post-testing of the treatment groups and involve appropriate comparison groups. The alternative, true *experimental designs* are designs that use random assignment for treatment. These designs are rare in education research.

Implications

A set of practitioner implications is presented at the close of each chapter. The number and variety of studies included in the chapter analyses suggest that these implications are relevant for other students who are performing below standards. In most cases the research does not provide evidence for the use of specific strategies, but there is collective evidence of which practitioners should be aware. This evidence is provided in levels based on the following guidelines:

• *The research suggests:* In many cases the available research reveals trends that support certain strategies or specific interventions for at-risk or low-performing students. The lack of extensive research (in terms of numbers of studies, numbers of studied participants, and study quality) in these areas, however, limits the confidence with which claims can be made. In these cases, the strategies or interventions are presented as "suggested" practices.

• *Strong evidence:* There are contexts in which a sufficient amount of high-quality research studies are available. In some of these contexts, the research clearly points to an intervention or strategy that should be used with at-risk or low-performing students. In these cases, the implications box leads with the phrase "the research supplies strong evidence that," followed by important strategies and interventions.

Readers who are accustomed to reading expert opinion may find the implications provided in this book to be comparatively less definitive. Please understand that this book presents only what careful research has to say about improving the achievement of at-risk students. That which is missing from these implications has not been proved to be effective for these students.

Discussion Guide

A Discussion Guide can be found at the end of this publication. This section is useful for practitioners who wish to compare the results of current research to their own practice. The guide is organized so that discussions can be organized around a single chapter topic or across a number of chapters. Questions are provided to provoke thought and conversation. Note that the guide also provides a quick summary of the availability of research and results under each chapter heading, so it can also serve as a synopsis of this book.

Reference

Barley, Z., Lauer, P. A., Arens, S. A., Apthorp, H. S., Englert, K. S., Snow, D., & Akiba, M. (2002). *Helping at-risk students meet standards: A synthesis of evidence-based classroom practices* (REL Deliverable #2002-20). Aurora, CO: Mid-continent Research for Education and Learning.

Chapter 1

Whole-Class
Instruction

In a multicultural 5th-grade classroom, the teacher has shifted from basal readers to a literature-based curriculum designed by her and a colleague. During reading instruction, she pushes her students to expand not only their vocabularies and knowledge of the world but also their ability to interpret what they read. For example, while reading two stories that center on the experiences of black Americans during the Revolutionary War, the class is assigned to write about fairness in the stories. Later, the students share the results of their efforts with each other. As the teacher guides the students in the presentation of their thoughts to peers, she teaches them how to compliment and support each other in a group setting. As the children read what they have written, the teacher finds something encouraging to say to each before offering constructive criticism and suggestions for expansion or rewriting. This teacher finds that having students write about what they have read facilitates comprehension. (Knapp, Shields, & Turnbull, 1992, p. 8)

T he set of observations on the opposite page was included in a national policy report aimed at the instruction of at-risk youth. Our notion of teachers working with a classroom full of students is a firm tradition in the United States, and, in this respect, the preceding description is of a typical classroom. The teacher is managing a class of young readers as they work through a reading lesson. We are not told how many students there are in this class, but the authors expect that we have a good idea. To us, a public school teacher is someone who is comfortable working with 20 to 30 (or more) students at a time. The teacher described here is one such teacher. She is not only keeping her class focused and instructing students in reading, but she is also working with them to develop character.

In This Chapter

- What the research has to say about whole-class instruction and at-risk student achievement

- An overview of *behaviorism* and *constructivism*

- Practitioner implications

Despite the availability of strategies such as cooperative learning, peer tutoring, and computer-aided instruction (strategies analyzed in later chapters of this book), teachers still rely heavily on instructing a classroom of students all at once. Good or bad, this is traditional education. And, because it is an important part of our tradition and practice, this kind of instruction is often studied by education researchers. The authors of the national policy report were preceded by many others, and many more have followed in the effort to study the relationship between classroom teaching and the achievement of at-risk students. These studies of traditional classroom instruction, or *whole-class instruction,* are analyzed in this chapter. Note that the contents of this chapter are a direct extension of Sheila Arens's General Instruction chapter in McREL's 2002 synthesis (Barley et al.) and that her work would be a good resource for those interested in more information about the current research on whole-class instruction of at-risk students.

Before taking a closer look at the whole-class instruction studies, however, it is important to understand the lens through which Arens analyzed the available studies. As one would expect, the studies present a wide variety of interventions, from a rote approach to early literacy (Marseglia, 1997) to a high school classroom management strategy designed to improve student performance across the curriculum (Morris, 1998). The wide range of programming brought to light by recent research limits the ability to draw specific comparisons about strategies because no two studies report on programs that are largely similar. Despite this variety, Arens was able to analyze the works through one broad characterization that makes some general and potentially useful comparisons possible. This broad characterization involves a close look at the constructivist and behaviorist theories underpinning each of the programs studied.

The opposition of the two theories has been raising questions in the minds of teachers for the last 20 or 30 years. Conflict arises because the theories are so thoroughly opposed in their perspectives and because the resulting practices are so different. Despite the potential for conflict, the constructivist–behaviorist debate has encouraged reflection and has helped more than a few teachers improve their practice. An analysis of available research viewed through a constructivist–behaviorist lens results in some research-based conclusions about this debate. After a discussion of constructivism, behaviorism, and the studies that were included in the McREL synthesis, the conclusions drawn by Arens are presented here as implications that can improve classroom practice.

A constructivist instructional practice is one that encourages students to come to their own understanding of the concept at hand. Constructivist theory not only challenges the traditional notion of learning as a steady progression of concepts, but also challenges the traditionally static notion of what it means to "know" something.[1] A good example of a potentially constructivist approach can be seen in the opening of this chapter. Initially the teacher discards the basal readers in favor of a presumably more divergent set of readings. Then she encourages students to use the readings as a basis for consideration and discussion around the topic of fairness. The reader expects that the students are

---

[1] *A very readable collection of constructivist essays is presented in* Constructivism: Theory, Perspectives, and Practice, *by Fosnot (1996).*

coming to personal understandings of the concept of fairness, which would be a goal of a constructivist lesson.

In contrast, behaviorism sees knowledge as a deliverable quantity. The behaviorist teacher is the classroom expert passing along knowledge to the student. The strongest

Balancing Phonics and Whole Language Instruction

In the 1980s and into the 1990s, behaviorists and constructivists engaged in a debate that boiled down to the use of phonics versus the use of whole language in early literacy instruction. In many cases the strong theoretical stance of the constructivists' *whole language* was challenged by the undeniable results produced by the behaviorists' *phonics* instruction. This became known as the Great Phonics Debate.

But much has been written over the past decade about a need for a balanced approach in teaching reading. A balanced approach is one that incorporates both phonics and whole language to best suit the needs of young readers. Advocates of a balanced approach see the strengths of a variety of instructional strategies. In 1998, the National Council of Teachers of English published two books that promoted a balanced approach (Weaver, 1998a and 1998b). Constance Weaver (1998b), the editor of these volumes, phrased it this way:

> I argue for instruction based on a coherent integration of the best of differing bodies and types of research and a theory of reading that puts meaning at the heart of reading from the very beginning, rather than as some distant goal. (p. 14)

As Weaver suggests, a balanced approach is supported by research. More recently this position was reinforced by the National Reading Panel (2000):

> . . . it is important to emphasize that systematic phonics instruction should be integrated with other reading instruction to create a balanced reading program. (p. 2-136)

McREL's synthesis of general classroom instruction research reinforces this position in two ways. First, the research indicates that there is not one unique and superior approach to reading instruction. Second, it appears as though successful instruction is dependent on using an approach that is best suited to the desired outcome. Given the variety of desired outcomes represented by reading standards, a mixed or balanced approach is certainly warranted.

defense of a behaviorist approach may be that it has been used with relative success for hundreds if not thousands of years.[2] In the opening passage, it becomes clear that the teacher begins to reveal some behaviorist strategies in addition to her initially constructivist tack. After asking students to write about a particular theme in the two stories and then providing time for students to share their work with one another, she makes suggestions for improvements and monitoring the interactions of the group. Her comments suggest that she is the expert and knows what they should write and how they should act, comments that reveal behaviorist beliefs.

It seems as though the teacher in the opening passage is presenting a lesson that effectively meets the needs of her at-risk students. She relies on both constructivist and behaviorist strategies in her effort to meet those needs, and she appears to strike an appropriate balance. In fact, many of the studies in this chapter describe and analyze programs that employ a constructivist–behaviorist balance in their efforts to serve students (see sidebar). Because these balanced approaches are making a deliberate attempt to infuse constructivist strategies into the longstanding behaviorist tradition, their studies are included in the constructivist discussion to follow.

Fifteen behaviorist and constructivist studies representing the achievement of more than 3,500 students were reviewed by Arens for McREL's synthesis of findings on effective strategies to assist low-achieving students in meeting standards. All of these studies contributed to the results and implications that appear in the following pages. Five of the studies, including the large-scale report of 140 classrooms introduced in the opening passage, inform conclusions about constructivist strategies as they are employed in whole-class instruction. The remaining 10 studies form the basis of a discussion on behaviorist whole-class instruction. All but one of the studies in this chapter relied on a quasi-experimental design, and many of the studies also yielded qualitative results through rich description and transcribed interactions.

---

[2] *An interesting discussion of the constancy of education beliefs can be found in Chapter 8 of* How Teachers Taught: Constancy and Change in American Classrooms 1880–1990, *by Cuban (1993).*

Program Review

In order to better contrast the opposing perspectives of constructivism and behaviorism, the studies of related programs are presented separately here. Despite the differences between the constructivist and behaviorist perspectives and the different strategies they encourage, it is important to remember that all of the studies drew conclusions about their strategies in terms of the academic achievement of the students involved. The goal in each case was to reveal effective ways to serve low-achieving students.

Constructivist Whole-Class Instruction

The five constructivist whole-class instruction research studies represent a variety of programs. In one program for 2nd graders in California (Sylva, 2000), the students use journals to improve their writing, while a 3rd- and 4th-grade program in Colorado (Wolf, 1998) has students involved in theater as a means to encourage and improve reading proficiency. A more balanced approach is employed by a program in the Southeast (Simmons, Fuchs, Fuchs, Mathes, & Hodges, 1995) that integrates direct, systematic instruction into a constructivist approach to elementary reading instruction.

In addition to student achievement gains, many of these studies reveal program characteristics in the form of transcribed conversations and activity descriptions. This is

Constructivist Skills

A program that encourages a skill such as journal writing, for example, can improve a student's ability to write creatively. Similarly, a program that encourages connections between text and past experience is shown to encourage the ability to interpret text.

Behaviorist Skills

The research also suggests that drill in math computation and spelling is shown to improve these behaviors. Marseglia's description on page 16 of the 1st graders reading *Moondance* is a good example of this relationship. The students' final assessment was directly related to the lesson activity, and most of the students demonstrated increased fluency.

Reflection Question

Are there subjects or topics that best lend themselves to students constructing their own understanding?

certainly the case in a study of the Students Achieving Independent Learning (SAIL) program (Brown, Pressley, Van Meter, & Schuder, 1996). The 2nd-grade low-achieving students in the program were taught to actively interpret and anticipate as they read. One focus of the SAIL students' efforts was to draw on personal experience in digesting the readings. Here is an excerpt from the study:

Student: In the story, um um, the frog was just laughing because it was a miracle that came true. And the frog was laughing, the frog was laughing at them. And then really really when he was talking he said, "Don't you know what happens when it rains over a mushroom?" And they they didn't know. They thought it was just a miracle, and when it was getting bigger it looked like a sleeping cap. So I think it was going wider and wider, and afterward when the sun came out and the fox was like an evil spirit, it went away. Um, they came, they came right out, and the mushroom was so big they didn't know what happened.

After the retelling was over, the researcher, curious about the origins of the student's interpretation, asked why he thought the fox was an evil spirit. The student replied:

Student: Because it's like you know, the movies. And once there's this evil spirit and it's dark and nothing happens right. And once you kill it, the evil spirit, or if it goes away, and then it turns back into a good life.

Thus, the student used his personal knowledge accrued from viewing movies to generate a unique interpretation that entered into his retelling. (p. 30)

It is difficult to discern the quality of the boy's understanding of the text based on this passage, but the passage does make it clear that he was able to make use of his experience in reaching an understanding. In reading the passage, one gets the sense that had he been told how to think about the story, he may not have interpreted the story the way he did. This window into a student's mind—his way of coming to know a text—is one example of constructivist theory that has been applied in a classroom. The studies presented in this chapter share many such examples along with test scores from students who have been exposed to such interventions. The results of these studies inform the implications to follow.

Behaviorist Whole-Class Instruction

A review of the 10 studies that focused on behaviorist whole-class instruction reveals a number of aggressive, methodical strategies aimed at remediating low-performing students. The language carries a familiar no-nonsense tone as the authors refer to filling in gaps, providing foundations, and helping students catch up to peers, while the methods varied widely from the use of mathematics flash cards (Su, 1990) to a broad campaign to improve reading interest and activity, including an effort to encourage library membership (Turner, 1993).

Most of the programs studied focused on improved reading for students with low ability or for those very young students identified to be at risk for having problems in their efforts to begin reading. A Texas program is typical of the group of reading interventions. This large study of 1st- and 2nd-grade Title I students (Foorman, Francis, Fletcher, Mehta, & Schatschneider, 1998) detailed the direct instruction in letter–sound correspondence and spelling patterns that was the core of the program. Two classes of urban students in Illinois, one kindergarten and one 5th-grade class, were exposed to a program that provided instruction in letter–sound association, decoding strategies, and phonics in another effort to improve reading proficiency (Hennenfent & Russell, 2001). In Maryland, kindergarten students who scored low on an assessment of reading readiness were channeled into a program designed to help them develop reading skills (George-Remy, 1991). The teacher-researcher designed an intervention that encouraged the students to reread stories in an effort to reach proficiency.

Behaviorist strategies often are easily described as a set of instructional steps that will lead students to understanding. The following passage is one such example. It is taken from a study of 1st-grade readers who scored below their average classmates in a local assessment (see Marseglia, 1997). The 20 students identified as low performers on this measure are taken through the following intervention:

> Individually, students were asked to read the story *Moondance*. No background information was given other than the title of the story. These readings were audio taped. If a student could not identify a word, the teacher supplied the word after a five second delay. Miscues, in the form of omissions, substitutions, mispronunciations, or insertions, were not corrected.

> After all students had read the story once for audio taping, the big book version of *Moondance* was shared with the whole class. Most students recognized the story from their attempts to read it. The story was discussed briefly before the story was read in its entirety as the teacher tracked the print with her finger and the children followed along. Further discussion followed this reading. The story was read a second time, and the children were invited to join in wherever they could.

> The next day, groups of six children listened to a commercially prepared audio tape of the story on headphones as they followed along in individual texts. This represented the third reading. No teacher assistance or involvement occurred.

> On the third day, students were paired with a peer according to their sight vocabulary scores. The lowest scoring student was paired with the highest scoring student, and subsequent students were paired in the same way. These pairs were asked to read the story together, sharing one book between them in order to prevent students from reading at their own pace and ignoring their partner. This procedure was not new to the students.

> On the fourth day, students were once again asked to read the story *Moondance* and were audio taped as they did. The same procedures were followed as during the first taping.

> The audio tapes of the first and final readings were analyzed for reading rate by determining the number of words per minute, and for word recognition, by determining the number of miscues. A score for correct words per minute was used to assess changes in fluency. (pp. 4–5)

The author is describing a lesson in which a teacher is taking advantage of a variety of groupings, but the overriding structure is one of activity at the classroom level. For this reason, and because any teacher could be directed to facilitate the described session without specific training in peer tutoring or cooperative learning, this studied program is presented as an example of a whole-class instructional intervention aimed at addressing the needs of low-performers.

The most important thing to note about this passage in light of the behaviorist–constructivist discussion is that there are several strongly behaviorist notions that carry through this passage. The most obvious of these is that repeated exposure to the story *Moondance* will result in an increased ability to read this book and others like it. The passage also reveals the importance of quantifiable measures in a behaviorist perspective: word counts, timed penalties, and numbers of miscues. After comparing the measures of fluency, the author concludes that the intervention is an effective one but notes that the lowest level readers in the study did not benefit as much as did their classmates.

Results

Two of the five constructivist studies, along with five of the 10 behaviorist studies, reported positive results in their studies of at-risk students. In this context, a positive result suggests that the studied program produced significant student growth in a measurable skill. For most of these studies, the measured skill was reading, which usually meant early literacy skills, while some of the programs focused on other skills such as writing and mathematics. The individual studies often prove interesting and may inform practice, but stronger results emerge from the group of studies considered as a whole. If a positive result is found in more than one instance, it provides some evidence that the common intervention may work in other settings.

The strongest theme that emerges from the whole-class instruction studies reviewed in this chapter is that the successful outcome of an intervention is most often aligned with the activity used to induce that outcome. In other words, the research consistently

reveals that an intervention of any sort has great potential to increase a student's performance in an activity or context that is similar to the achievement measure.

It is worth noting that a broad analysis of constructivist or behaviorist approaches suggests that neither is superior to the other. Even when the practices are measured against typical academic standards, there is no one clear, successful approach or strategy that emerges. Teachers are left to believe either that the research has yet to uncover the superior approach in the constructivist–behaviorist debate or that the strategies each have their places in effective teaching. This second option is supported by the fact that the available research indicates a relationship between the instructional method and effective student learning. Decisions regarding behaviorist and constructivist teaching strategies should be guided by the desired outcome. Coming to this conclusion frees the teacher to use a variety of constructivist or behaviorist strategies—and supports the variety that many practitioners already employ—in order to meet the needs of their low-performing students.

Beyond merely choosing the strategy to use in a given situation, teachers may find that the most effective approach is one that takes advantage of both constructivist and behaviorist strategies. In practice, it is actually quite difficult to avoid a combination of these strategies. Even the most thoroughly constructivist interventions described in the research were peppered with behaviorist practices, and the converse was also true. Again returning to the *Moondance* passage (Marseglia, 1997), the activity illustrates a thoroughly behaviorist lesson while allotting time for discussion. Why discuss? This teacher, in seeing the importance of discussion as a part of an effective lesson, was displaying a constructivist tendency within an otherwise behaviorist approach. As noted earlier (see sidebar on page 11), the most effective combinations of constructivist and behaviorist strategies are referred to as balanced instruction.

Clearly, more research is needed in identifying effective instructional strategies and in comparing these strategies to the strategies cited in the other chapters of this book. The following implications are offered, although not supported by strong research evidence.

Implications

Whole-class instruction is defined here as any intervention that involves the teacher delivering a lesson to a classroom of students all at one time. The available research studies comparing these interventions to resulting achievement gains, although limited in number, were analyzed in terms of each intervention's constructivist or behaviorist framework. The following implications for working with low-achieving or at-risk students are the result:

The research suggests that . . .

> . . . when choosing specific teaching strategies in any context, the desired outcome should guide the instructional decisions (for example, a behavioral outcome such as spelling should encourage a behaviorist lesson, while a more constructivist outcome such as writing should encourage a constructivist lesson).

> . . . constructivist strategies are not generally superior to behaviorist strategies and behaviorist strategies are not generally superior to constructivist strategies, and there is no indication that either should be used exclusively.

> . . . searching for an appropriate balance between constructivist and behaviorist strategies may be the best approach to effective intervention.

References

Barley, Z., Lauer, P. A., Arens, S. A., Apthorp, H. S., Englert, K. S., Snow, D., & Akiba, M. (2002). *Helping at-risk students meet standards: A synthesis of evidence-based classroom practices* (REL Deliverable #2002-20). Aurora, CO: Mid-continent Research for Education and Learning. Available online at www.mcrel.org

Brown, R., Pressley, M., Van Meter, P., & Schuder, T. (1996). A quasi-experimental validation of transactional strategies instruction with low-achieving second-grade readers. *Journal of Educational Psychology, 88*(1), 18–37.

Cuban, L. (1993). *How teachers taught: Constancy and change in American classrooms 1880–1990.* New York: Teachers College Press.

Foorman, B. R., Francis, D. J., Fletcher, J. M., Mehta, P., & Schatschneider, C. (1998). The role of instruction in learning to read: Preventing reading failure in at-risk children. *Journal of Educational Psychology, 90*(1), 37–55.

Fosnot, C. (1996). *Constructivism: Theory, perspectives, and practice.* New York: Teachers College Press.

George-Remy, C. Y. (1991). Improvement in kindergarten children's expressions with the language arts: Short-term instruction on the parts of a story and story re-telling with teacher feedback. *Early Child Development & Care, 73,* 19–27.

Hennenfent, M., & Russell, J. (2001). *Increasing independent reading levels using an integrated approach emphasizing direct reading instruction.* Unpublished master's thesis, St. Xavier University, Chicago.

Knapp, M. S., Shields, P. M., & Turnbull, B. J. (1992). *Academic challenge for the children of poverty: Study of academic instruction for disadvantaged children. Summary report.* Washington, DC: U.S. Department of Education, Office of Policy and Planning.

Marseglia, P. (1997). The effect of repeated readings on the fluency of high and low level ability readers in a first grade class. Unpublished master's thesis, Kean College of New Jersey.

Morris, L. L. (1998). *The effects of integrated curriculum on 9th grade at-risk students.* Unpublished master's thesis, St. Xavier University, Chicago.

National Reading Panel. (2000). *Teaching children to read: An evidence-based assessment of the scientific research literature on reading and its implications for reading instruction. Reports of the subgroups.* Washington, DC: Author.

Simmons, D. C., Fuchs, L. S., Fuchs, D., Mathes, P., & Hodges, J. P. (1995). Effects of explicit teaching and peer tutoring on the reading achievement of learning-disabled and low-performing students in regular classrooms. *The Elementary School Journal, 95*(5), 387–408.

Su, H. F. H. (1990). Increasing fourth grade math achievement with improved instructional strategies. Unpublished doctoral dissertation, Nova University, Florida.

Sylva, J. A. (2000). Teaching literacy skills to students at risk: A writing intervention. *Dissertation Abstracts International, 60*(12-A), 4323. (UMI No. 9954165)

Turner, T. N. (1993). Improving reading comprehension achievement of sixth, seventh, and eighth grade underachievers. Unpublished doctoral dissertation, Nova University, Florida.

Weaver, C. (Ed.) (1998a). *Practicing what we know: Informed reading instruction.* Urbana, IL: National Council of Teachers of English.

Weaver, C. (Ed.) (1998b). *Reconsidering a balanced approach to reading.* Urbana, IL: National Council of Teachers of English.

Wolf, S. A. (1998). The flight of reading: Shifts in instruction, orchestration, and attitudes through classroom theatre. *Reading Research Quarterly, 33*(4), 382–415.

Chapter 2

Cognitively Oriented
Instruction

Teacher: Jean, you did not show how to change a ratio to a percent in a consistent manner. In problem 3 you divided the numerator by 100, in problem 4 you divided the numerator by the denominator, and in problem 5 you wrote a solution that does not correspond to either of the two previous procedures. Which procedure is correct? (Cardelle-Elawar, 1990, p. 170)

T
he opposite quote comes from a teacher who is speaking to a low-performing 6th-grade mathematics student. The student has just completed a set of problems that asked her to calculate a percent. The teacher is practicing skills learned in a course that encourages a metacognitive approach to mathematics instruction (Cardelle-Elawar, 1990). The goal of the teacher's question is to encourage Jean to consider a series of general problem-solving steps as the student works to solve math problems. In this case, the student is being encouraged to think critically about her results. The teacher is setting an example for Jean by asking which procedure is the correct one, and by doing so she is suggesting that Jean has not carefully reviewed the consistency of her solution steps. The teacher is hoping that Jean will come away from this experience with not only a better understanding of the specific process of converting ratios to percents, but also an increased ability to solve any number of other mathematic problems.

In This Chapter

• What the research has to say about cognitive and metacognitive strategies and at-risk student achievement

• Specific applications in mathematics, reading, and writing

• Practitioner implications

Cardelle-Elawar's study is one of the studies considered by Apthorp for McREL's 2000 research synthesis (Barley et al., 2002) in her study of cognitively oriented interventions. Apthorp's synthesis of the available research is presented in this chapter. Each of the studies looks at the connection between some cognitive strategy and the resulting achievement of the students who participated in the study. These strategies are expected to help students think about how they learn and to become better learners. The most effective interventions of this type will affect student performance in a wide variety of contexts and content areas. Proponents of these strategies suggest that cognitively oriented approaches not only assist students in meeting standards but also prepare them to be lifelong learners.

In this chapter, as in Apthorp's work, cognitively oriented strategies will be reviewed in two groups: *cognitive strategies* and *metacognitive strategies.* What are cognitive and metacognitive strategies? Cognitive strategies are those that strictly address how a student goes about learning. "How-to" approaches such as mathematics problem-solving strategies along with other direct, step-by-step approaches fall into this group. Unfortunately, directly improving cognition is difficult, so teachers often turn to metacognitive strategies. A metacognitive strategy is one step removed from a cognitive approach. The goal of a metacognitive approach is to improve the conditions for cognition. Metacognitive strategies "involve thinking about one's own thinking and task demands" (Barley et al., 2002, pp. 33–34). Strategies that encourage planning, preparation, and idea generation, as well as monitoring, self-checking, and revising, are each examples of metacognitive approaches.

Reading and Literacy

In a general sense, the most important metacognitive skill is the ability to read. Reading is the foundation for most academic pursuits, a fact that explains the focus on early literacy in the nation's effort to meet the needs of low-performing students.

Educators are accustomed to seeing the terms "reading" and "literacy" being used interchangeably (in the preceding paragraph, for example). Some researchers, however, prefer to make a distinction between the terms. For example, Pearson and Raphael (1999) suggest that "reading" is merely the act of interpreting and comprehending text, while "literacy" goes beyond text comprehension to an understanding of the text in relation to society.

Rueda and McIntyre (2002) illustrate this point by describing a young reader who is touched by a short story he reads while confined to his bed with a broken leg. The short story, the authors report, is not merely understood by the boy but rather internalized by him as he comes to terms with it in comparison to his confined state. This is literacy. The boy allowed his understanding of the text to mingle with his understanding of his world, and his literacy then became a tool with which he could learn much more than he could by just reading.

Note that these descriptions may give the false impression that there is a clear distinction between cognitive and metacognitive strategies. In fact, definitions of these strategies appear to be evolving; strategies once thought to be cognitive are now deemed to be metacognitive (see Dickson, Collins, Simmons, & Kameenui, 1998). Nonetheless, the general definitions of cognitive and metacognitive approaches provided here serve the purposes of reporting the results found by Apthorp and provide needed clarity in the implications to follow.

It is also important to note that the cognitive strategies reviewed in this chapter can certainly be applied in small groups, in peer tutoring, in computer-aided instruction, or in tutoring—the various grouping strategies that characterize the other chapters of this book. In fact, the opening passage of this chapter could easily describe an interaction between a tutor and tutee. This is not the case, however, and the research does not reveal the explicit use of these strategies in a variety of settings. The research reports the use of these strategies only in whole-class instructional settings. Given the research on these strategies in whole-class settings, this chapter on cognitively oriented strategies becomes a useful follow-up to the whole-class instruction strategies presented in the previous chapter.

Findings from 14 studies were synthesized by Apthorp. The interventions studied ranged in size from a group of 14 low-achieving 4th-grade students to a much larger study involving 108 at-risk 3rd and 5th graders. All of these studies were based on quasi-experimental designs averaging nearly 50 students in each of the treatment groups. In each study the resulting academic achievement of the students who participated in the programs was compared to that of similar students who did not participate in the studied programs. The programmatic comparisons and combined results of these studies inform the results reported by Apthorp and are presented in this chapter.

Program Review

For most of the classroom strategies discussed in this book, the subject-area differences are relatively few. An intervention that appears to be effective in reading, for example, appears to be similarly effective for math. But there are exceptions, and a review of the cognitively oriented research uncovers one such case.

One subject-area difference can be illustrated by a look back to the opening passage of this chapter. The student, Jean, is encouraged to take advantage of an analytical approach that will serve her well in solving the problem at hand, as well as thinking about a wide variety of problems. But she will find that the specific logic she is using is best suited for mathematics problem solving. This notion—that cognitive and meta-cognitive strategies are primarily content specific despite their potential to enhance learning—is a recurring theme in the research. And, because the use of cognitive and metacognitive approaches seems susceptible to broad changes in curricular context, the available research was separated with respect to content area. In the following sections, the studies of cognitive and metacognitive strategies are presented in the programmatic groups of reading, writing, and mathematics.

Reading Instruction

Nine studies of reading programs were reviewed. Six of these studies reported encouraging results for low-performing students. The strategies used in these six studies of successful programs, when contrasted with the interventions of the programs reported as being unsuccessful, suggest an interesting trend within the variety of approaches.

Reading Instruction: Drawing on the Research

1. Preview the text, for example, map or code the text.

2. Read the text.

3. Summarize the text, for example, write reactions or summaries of the text, or engage in some other form of expression such as drawing text images or acting out sections of the text.

Successful reading comprehension seems to be encouraged by any of a number of strategies aimed at situating the text within an established framework. The programs studied encourage students to identify certain characteristics (voice, genre, purpose, and themes, for example), to code the text in a variety of different ways (i.e., physically mark the text as a form of visual organization), or even to create visual maps of the text content (e.g., reorganize the text into a separate and more familiar format).

In the Northeast, a set of these strategies including genre identi-fication, and the use of predictions and summarizing, produced positive results among low-achieving 2nd graders (see Brown, Pressley, Van Meter, & Schuder, 1995). A southeastern program called "REAP" (Read, Encode, Annotate, Ponder) that relies on a series of cognitive and metacognitive steps implied in its name is reported by Brown (1995) to have had positive effects.

Reflection Question

What cognitive and metacognitive skills are taught in today's classrooms?

Another program similar to these produced positive effects in a Montana high school by encouraging students to map story concepts and to paraphrase the text (see Jakupcak, Rushton, Jakupcak, & Lundt, 1996).

In fact, there is a combination of strategies common to all of the successful reading programs, a combination absent in those programs reported to be unsuccessful. This combination begins with some effort to preview the text (a metacognitive strategy such as mapping or coding) and is followed, after the text has been read, by some effort to summarize (using a cognitive strategy involving writing or some other form of expression). Interventions that successfully encourage students to consider text in this way appear to be effective in encouraging comprehension.

Writing Instruction

There are three available studies of writing instruction programs that rely on cognitively oriented strategies. In each of these studies, the implementation is shown to be effective in demonstrating improved student achievement. Although the number of research studies is small, there is merit in attempting to recognize emerging trends. This is particularly true in light of the consistency among the results of the available reading research.

One of these studies focused on a Michigan program involving 52 low-achieving 4th and 5th graders (see Englert, Raphael, Anderson, Anthony, & Stevens, 1991). These students were taught to ask themselves a series of questions that would guide them in drafting a composition. This "how-to" or cognitive phase was supported by instructional conversations about writing strategies, and eventually by revising and editing encouraged by peer feedback.

> **Writing Instruction: Drawing on the Research**
>
> 1. Generate text; for example, write a first draft, or expand on a topic.
>
> 2. Make significant text revisions; for example, collect feedback, submit to formative evaluation, or conduct self-assessment.

This intervention was quite similar to that of a middle school program that helped 18 students improve their ability to write opinion essays (see Wong, Butler, Ficzere, & Kuperis, 1996). The authors describe an intervention that begins with writing essays, but then centers around a set of metacognitive questions, for example, "What things does a person have to know to become a good writer?" or "What goes on in your head when you write?" Again, the intervention is reported to produce positive results.

In a third study, 23 Maryland 9th graders who had failed a state writing assessment were encouraged to build their writing skills through a process that divided their conceptualization of the writing task into four components: topic, audience, purpose, and form (see Ketter & Pool, 2001). Subsequently, all but one of the students passed the state assessment, but the authors report that the process—the metacognitive planning sequence—seemed to stifle the students' creativity.

In considering these three studies of writing instruction, it is interesting to note that, like the research related to reading, a successful combination of strategies seems to emerge. But, in this case, the cognitive/metacognitive order appears to be reversed. The results of these three studies suggest that a successful combination of writing strategies should begin with an effort to generate text (a cognitive process such as draft writing or expanding on a topic in writing) followed by significant text revision (a metacognitive strategy or set of strategies such as collecting feedback, formative evaluation, or self-assessment).

Mathematics Instruction

Only two studies of mathematics instruction were available for discussion in this chapter. As was true of the writing research in cognitively oriented strategies, this pair of studies in mathematics is not adequate to support solid implications. But again, the programmatic similarities leading to comparable results are intriguing and worthy of mention.

Mathematics Instruction: Drawing on the Research

1. First, encourage students to recognize patterns in their problem solving, for example, by comparing the situation to similar problems and solutions.

2. Then give students opportunities to test these patterns.

One of the two mathematics studies is that of the program cited in the opening passage (see Cardelle-Elawar, 1990). The 80 6th-grade math students in this study were encouraged by their teachers to recognize patterns in their problem solving. This encouragement took the form of a set of metacognitive strategies that the students had been taught to use. As a result, most of the students showed significant improvement in their ability to solve similar problems. In the second study, 17 low-achieving students in a Wisconsin program also were encouraged to recognize patterns in math problems and attained a similar level of success (see Bottge, 1999). But the difference between the two interventions is that the Wisconsin teens were situated in a project-based context. The students in this study were motivated by an interest in building a skateboard ramp. Regardless of the context, however, the students in both of these studies were moved to focus on the process of problem solving, and the intervention resulted in an increased ability to solve other problems.

Results

Any confidence in results from the collection of studies reviewed in this chapter is muted by the small amount of research available. It is interesting, however, that some specific strategic combinations seem to be working for those who are implementing cognitive and metacognitive approaches. With this in mind, there are some results that show promise as general trends. Because the following results seem to be consistent within the programs studied, the emerging trends seen here should encourage further study.

The strongest research-based claim to be made in this chapter is the suggestion that cognitive/metacognitive reading instruction should coincide with a combination that encourages planning before reading, and is followed by some effort to summarize the text. The available research includes several examples of programs that display this combination successfully as well as several unsuccessful programs that omit one of the two steps.

The available research on cognitively oriented writing instruction is limited. There are three writing studies included here, all of which showed improved student achievement. A comparison of their program characteristics reveals what may be an important trend. Here, too, a combination of strategies seems to be encouraging student growth. Successful interventions tend to put initial effort into generating text and ideas, and then into significant student or peer assessments and revisions.

As was seen in the review of the writing research, the mathematics research also was limited. The available research included two studies that were similar in approach and were similarly successful. In each case the implementation taught students to consider patterns and use those patterns to solve a set of problems. In one study, the teacher served as a coach to facilitate this reflection; in the other study, students were motivated by their interest in the construction activity at hand. It was the nature of the activity in this second study that encouraged students to solve a number of problems. Regardless of the source of the motivation, encouraging students to think about similar approaches to similar problems seems to be a worthy goal in building mathematics problem-solving skills.

These results do suggest the possibility that successful outcome-specific cognitive or metacognitive strategies, or combinations of strategies, may emerge from research. For example, it may become clear that reading instruction is most effective when approached through a combination of strategies that begins with a metacognitive strategy and is followed by a cognitive strategy.

Implications

Research on using cognitive and metacognitive strategies in meeting the needs of low-achieving students is limited and does not, therefore, support a set of specific interventions. However, there are trends emerging from the studies that may be useful to practitioners working with at-risk students:

The research suggests that . . .

> . . . in reading instruction, a metacognitive strategy of planning (such as coding text) before reading, followed by an effort of summarizing, may be the most effective approach.

> . . . in writing instruction, a cognitive strategy of content creation (such as drafting) followed by a metacognitve strategy (such as self-assessment) may be the most effective approach.

> . . . in mathematics instruction, a metacognitive strategy of pattern recognition (mainly comparison to similar problems and solutions) followed by opportunities to test patterns may be the most effective approach.

References

Barley, Z., Lauer, P. A., Arens, S. A., Apthorp, H. S., Englert, K. S., Snow, D., & Akiba, M. (2002). *Helping at-risk students meet standards: A synthesis of evidence-based classroom practices* (REL Deliverable #2002-20). Aurora, CO: Mid-continent Research for Education and Learning. Available online at www.mcrel.org

Bottge, B. A. (1999). Effects of contextualized math instruction on problem solving of average and below-average achieving students. *The Journal of Special Education, 33*(2), 81–92.

Brown, D. M. (1995). Assisting eighth-grade at-risk students in successfully reading their textbooks through support strategies. Unpublished practicum report. Nova Southeastern University, Florida.

Brown, R., Pressley, M., Van Meter, P., & Schuder, T. (1995). *A quasi-experimental validation of transactional strategies instruction with previously low-achieving, second-grade readers* (Reading Research Report No. 33). Universities of Georgia and Maryland, National Reading Research Center.

Cardelle-Elawar, M. (1990). Effects of feedback tailored to bilingual students' mathematics needs on verbal problem solving. *The Elementary School Journal, 91*(2), 165–170.

Dickson, S. V., Collins, V. L., Simmons, D. C., & Kameenui, E. J. (1998). Metacognitive strategies: Research bases. In D. C. Simmons & E. J. Kameenui (Eds.), *What reading research tells us about children with diverse learning needs: Bases and basics* (pp. 295–360). Mahwah, NJ: Erlbaum.

Englert, C. S., Raphael, T. E., Anderson, L. M., Anthony, H. M., & Stevens, D. D. (1991). Making strategies and self-talk visible: Writing instruction in regular and special education classrooms. *American Educational Research Journal, 28*(2), 337–372.

Jakupcak, J., Rushton, R., Jakupcak, M., & Lundt, J. (1996). Inclusive education. *The Science Teacher, 63*(5), 40–43.

Ketter, J., & Pool, J. (2001). Exploring the impact of a high-stakes direct writing assessment in two high school classrooms. *Research in the Teaching of English, 35,* 344–393.

Pearson, P. D., & Raphael, T. E. (1999). Toward a more complex view of balance in the literacy curriculum. In W. D. Hammond & T. E. Raphael (Eds.), *Early literacy instruction for the new millennium* (pp. 1–21). Grand Rapids, MI: Michigan Reading Association.

Rueda, R., & McIntyre, E. (2002). Toward universal literacy. In S. Stringfield & D. Land (Eds.), *Educating at-risk students* (pp. 189–209). Chicago, IL: University of Chicago Press.

Wong, B. Y. L., Butler, D. L., Ficzere, S. A., & Kuperis, S. (1996). Teaching low achievers and students with learning disabilities to plan, write, and revise opinion essays. *Journal of Learning Disabilities, 29*(2), 197–212.

Chapter 3

Small
Groups

The following exchange is one example taken from the research. These four children have just finished a science reading on the skeletal system in their 5th-grade classroom. Tasha, the first student to speak, reads a question provided by her teacher:

Tasha: What might happen if your bones did not contain enough calcium?

Luis: They will break.

Tasha: OK, they will probably break. But can we add a little bit?

Roland: Well, first of all, what is calcium? And then we can figure out what it says and how it helps the bones.

Luis: OK, calcium is something that keeps the bones healthy and stuff like that.

Erica: Tasha?

Tasha: If you don't have enough calcium the bones will rot and you will be dead. And, then after you die you know your bones decay and you turn into dust. Your bones will like decompose in your body which will destroy and corrupt. If it does not have enough calcium, then the bones will get weak and break.

Erica: OK, I would say the same thing because the bones without calcium are nothing.

Roland: All right, well, we finished this. (Klinger & Vaughn, 2000, p. 85)

Organizing students to work in small groups is a fairly common practice. Being told that students were placed in small groups does not, however, reveal the nature or quality of their learning. There is great variety in the characteristics and goals of these groups, as well as the designs of the lessons. A look at the available research sheds light on these differences and what we know about the overall value of small groups as an instructional strategy for at-risk or low-performing students. The variety of interventions studied and the resulting effects on the performance of low-performing students are the focus of this chapter.

In This Chapter

• What the research has to say about small-group instruction and at-risk student achievement

• Issues related to *mixed-ability* and *like-ability* grouping

• Practitioner implications

The low-achieving students in the opening example took part in an intervention that encouraged them to work together to improve their reading comprehension. The study authors, Klinger and Vaughn (2000), refer to the intervention as "collaborative strategic reading," which is their specific extension of the small-group approach known as *cooperative learning*. The groups were asked to read and then discuss their readings within a provided framework. The study reported significant gains for all of the students involved in the intervention.

Before looking at other studies, it is important to note that it is one particular characteristic—the mixed-ability or like-ability groupings—that was the focus of Englert's analysis for McREL's 2002 research synthesis (Barley et al., 2002). The potential influence of mixed-ability grouping is illustrated by the small group described in the opening passage. We notice that the four students clearly represent a variety of abilities within their classroom. Tasha, for example, appears to be a 5th-grade expert on calcium and bones. But it also appears from the exchange that the students were asked to play a variety of roles. For example, it appears as though Roland was asked to play an organizational role in the activity and that Tasha was encouraged to help others come to an understanding of the concepts at hand. The students were placed in mixed-ability groups intentionally, and they were encouraged to play a variety of roles and to help one another toward understanding. Englert's work as presented here sheds light on the significance of mixed-ability groupings, such as this one, as well as like-ability grouping choices.

In addition to providing an example of small-group interactions, the opening passage also serves as a good example of a cooperative learning strategy. Cooperative learning is a specifically defined intervention, but is just one example of the grouping choices available to classroom teachers. Other mixed-ability designs and some like-ability grouping designs also are represented in the available research. A sense of the programs studied follows in the review of the 18 quasi-experimental studies that inform the results presented in this chapter. On average, each of the studies exposed 74 students[1] to some small-group intervention and then compared these results to those of comparison groups of students. This review focuses on the strategies and activity descriptions that were studied and what we know about their effectiveness.

Program Review

A review of the available research yields a natural classification of the studies into two categories:

- *Mixed-Ability Groupings:* Mixed-ability groupings also are referred to as "heterogeneous" grouping because the students within each group are dissimilar with regard to ability.

- *Like-Ability Groupings:* Like-ability groups are commonly referred to as "ability groupings" or "homogeneous groups" because the students within each group are relatively similar with regard to ability.

---

[1] *The calculation of this average does not include one large-scale analysis (n=3,991) of TIMSS (Third International Mathematics and Science Study) data presented by Bode (1996).*

Although the differences between these two categories may seem superficial, the implications of a teacher's decision to use one or the other run much deeper. At the heart of the issue is how best to serve those in the classroom who are at risk of failure. Should those who are most at risk be placed in groups where their more advanced peers can help them to succeed? Or should these at-risk students work together in small groups where they will all be working at the same level and supporting one another? A closer look at each choice should help to answer these questions.

Mixed-Ability Groupings

Ten of the small-group research studies reviewed by Englert centered on the effects of mixed-ability groupings. All of the programs studied in this group relied on practices that can be described as being consistent with the established characteristics of effective cooperative learning: clearly defined tasks, encouraged interaction within the group, and differentiation of group roles (see Johnson, Johnson, Holubec, & Roy, 1984). Most of the interventions seem to encourage students to use the group as a means to accomplish tasks more effectively and, in many cases, appear to be meeting the needs of the low-achievers in the groups.

In California, one program incorporated cooperative learning groups into a 7th-grade math classroom (see Webb & Farivar, 1994), while another program for middle school students used cooperative learning groups to reinforce math concepts along with the use of manipulatives (see Henderson & Landesman, 1992). The teachers in these classrooms facilitated learning by framing the activities, encouraging appropriate interactions, and serving as coaches. Both of the studies reported significant gains among most of the low-achieving students involved in cooperative learning groups when compared to those who were not involved in the groups.

Interestingly, computers were used in cooperative learning groups in three of the programs studied. A Pennsylvania study used computers to encourage math achievement for a group of 40 8th-grade students identified as being in need of additional support (see Hooper & Hannafin, 1988). A middle school science lesson was supported by another use of computers and cooperative groupings (see Singhanayok & Hooper, 1998). In this case, the groups were given access to a computer-based ecology tutorial as a reference source for their work. A third, similar intervention was used to help low-achieving 7th graders in a Texas program (see Repman, 1993). These students worked in cooperative groups supported by social studies software. An aim of this program was to frame an activity that would encourage analytical discussion about the social studies curriculum. Each of these three studies reported academic growth for the students involved in the interventions.

A group of 75 2nd-grade students in a midwestern elementary school were part of a study that compared three groups: a small set of cooperative learning groups that were provided with a guide for their discussions, a comparably sized set of cooperative learning groups that did not have a guide for structured discussion, and a group of students who received general instruction (see Yager, Johnson, & Johnson, 1985). The study authors report that not only did both of the cooperative learning groups encourage more academic growth in comparison to the results of the general instruction group, but also that by encouraging structured discussion, teachers were able to further increase levels of performance. The authors suggest that developing discussion guides is an important step in preparing for the lesson.

Like-Ability Groupings

The available research on like-ability grouping programs indicates that, when students do end up in like-ability groups, it is not typically the result of a conscious effort by a teacher to divide the class into groups by ability—one group of the lowest ability, one of the next lowest, and so on. Instead, like-ability groupings tend to be the result of two different attempts to meet the needs of low-achieving students. The first of these is that all of the students in a given class are at risk or low achieving, which leaves the teacher with no choice in the matter. Groupings in a class of this sort are destined to be like-ability at a low level. Second, low-achieving students are often identified within mixed-ability classes and provided extra help in small groups. These small groups are also low-level like-ability groupings. A review of several studies further illustrates the nature of these programs and the challenges they face.

Two studies of elementary students illustrate the use of small groups in a class full of low-achieving students, as well as the difficulties associated with attempting to bring a whole class of at-risk students up to achievement standards. The first of these studies (see Bruce, Snodgrass, & Salzman, 1999) describes a group of 1st graders in Ohio who were divided into small groups and given a guided reading lesson. The additional structure imposed by the intervention (and a great deal of teacher effort) reportedly resulted in academic growth. In a similar intervention, a class of 3rd-grade writing students in Virginia was divided into two groups in order to facilitate the sharing of ideas (see Colby, Parker, & Wilson, 1995). Again, the restructuring of the class and added structure, this time in the form of added staffing, appear to be the reason for the intervention's success.

In classrooms with students of mixed abilities, the problem of meeting the needs of relatively fewer at-risk students is clearer but no easier to solve. By first identifying low-performing students and then placing them in small groups, the studied interventions isolate the students with the greatest academic needs. But what is to be done with the rest of the class? And what will the low-performers miss? The available research is vague with respect to these questions. It does appear, however, that the needs of the low-performers are met with either additional staffing, additional teacher effort, and/or carefully designed activities.

This situation is illustrated by the study of a large "pull-in" program in Utah that solved the problem of meeting the needs of low-performing middle schoolers by bringing paraprofessionals into their mixed-ability classrooms to work with the low-achievers in reading and math (see Welch, Richards, Okada, Richards, & Prescott, 1995). In an Illinois program,

Tracking

When a teacher chooses to separate a class into like- or mixed-ability groups, the teacher is making a choice that may have unintended consequences. Like-ability groups elevate some students to the "high group" and leave others in the "low group." In this case, the teacher needs to weigh the opportunity to remediate low-performers against the possibility that the low-performers may be entering a trajectory of low performance from which they will not escape.

The question is when it is appropriate to begin tracking students, or even if it is appropriate to track students at all. In an international study of tracking, LeTendre, Hofer, and Shimizu (2003) report that ability tracking exists in every industrialized nation, but that this seemingly accepted international practice is seen differently in different countries. Japan and Germany, for example, begin tracking in later grades. The authors suggest that the practice in the United States of tracking students in early elementary school is more likely to limit the potential for success of at-risk students.

The issue of tracking is an important one in any discussion on within-class ability grouping. There is a wealth of tracking research available, and the recent LeTendre et al. study provides a good place to start.

identified at-risk kindergarten students were provided with small-group instruction in phonological and phonemic awareness and literacy acquisition (see Hawley, 2001). Classroom teachers provide similar supplementary instruction to their elementary students in North Carolina (see Morris & Nelson, 1992) and Michigan (see Palinscar, Brown, & Campione, 1989). All of these studies reported increased performance of their at-risk and identified low-performing students.

Results

Broad comparisons of the mixed-ability grouping interventions lead to the two important results identified by Englert. The first of these results is that the intervention can be successful. The research provides a number of examples of successful interventions that are situated in a variety of classroom settings. This group of studies, in addition to the publications that provide guidance in the design and facilitation of cooperative learning sessions, provide a wealth of resources for practitioners. Practitioners who have not been exposed to books on cooperative learning would do well to start with *Circles of Learning* (Johnson, Johnson, Holubec, & Roy, 1984) or *Cooperative Learning: Theory, Research, and Practice* (Slavin, 1995).

Reflection Question

How important are small groups to an effective learning environment?

The second important result that emerges from the mixed-ability studies is the strong sense that the quality of the planning and intervention is critical to the success of the intervention. The studies of successful interventions repeatedly emphasize the need for one or more of the following: careful attention to activity preparation (materials and space), careful attention to activity design (materials, interesting contexts or problems, and lesson flow), and efforts to encourage deep student discussion (carefully designed questions or assignments). It follows from these observations that staff training must also be an important part of an implementation given the complexity of the facilitator role.

Although it is difficult to make quantifiable claims with regard to the quality of the intervention and its effect on achievement based on the research, when the reader looks at the studies from a practical standpoint it does become clear that the role of the teacher is well defined in successful mixed-ability interventions. Most of the research on effective practice indicates that the efforts of the teacher are focused on a careful design prior to the small-group experience, and then on maintaining the learning environment throughout the session. The importance of preparation and implementation may lie in the fact that the mixed-ability group teacher is one step removed from a traditional role. Whereas the teacher is often coaching students in a traditional classroom setting, a mixed-ability teacher is often coaching students who are teaching others.

Unfortunately for teachers of classes that are filled with low-achieving students, mixed-ability grouping is not a reasonable option. Grouping strategies for these teachers is limited to like-ability small groups. The research also brings to light situations in which low-performing or at-risk students are separated from the class in an effort to remediate and close gaps. By nature of this action, these students, too, are placed in like-ability groups.

Like-ability groupings can be successful. As was true in the mixed-ability research, it is also true that the quality of the intervention is related to a positive result. But the availability of high-quality, like-ability research on groupings is limited. The lack of evidence from research leaves too many questions unanswered. Teachers need to know what resources—how many more staff, what kinds of structured activities—are needed in order for them to use small groups effectively in their classes full of low-performers. And what happens when low-performers are pulled out of class activities? What activities are they missing? More questions arise: What level of success can be expected? How will like-ability grouping affect high-performing students in the class? Research that results in reliable answers to these questions is needed in this area.

Implications

The research suggests that . . .

. . . mixed-ability grouping can be an effective strategy in meeting the needs of at-risk and low-achieving students. This is particularly true when the basic tenets of cooperative learning are followed.

. . . quality in staff training, activity preparation, and activity facilitation appears to be a necessary prerequisite to the success of the mixed-ability sessions.

. . . like-ability grouping has not been as thoroughly studied in the recent research. The available research in this area suggests a positive effect but lacks the rigor necessary to use it as a basis for suggested practice.

References

Barley, Z., Lauer, P. A., Arens, S. A., Apthorp, H. S., Englert, K. S., Snow, D., & Akiba, M. (2002). *Helping at-risk students meet standards: A synthesis of evidence-based classroom practices* (REL Deliverable #2002-20). Aurora, CO: Mid-continent Research for Education and Learning. Available online at www.mcrel.org

Bode, R. K. (1996, April). *Is it ability grouping or the tailoring of instruction that makes a difference in student achievement?* Paper presented at the annual meeting of the American Educational Research Association, New York.

Bruce, C., Snodgrass, D., & Salzman, J. A. (1999, October). *A tale of two methods: Melding Project Read and Guided Reading to improve at-risk students' literacy skills.* Paper presented at the annual meeting of the Mid-Western Educational Research Association, Chicago.

Colby, R. G., Parker, A. K., & Wilson, M. A. (1995). *Experienced-based writing and the at-risk student.* Washington, DC: ERIC.

Hawley, M. A. (2001). *A balanced literacy approach incorporating phonological awareness in kindergarten.* Unpublished doctoral dissertation, St. Xavier University, Chicago.

Henderson, R. W., & Landesman, E. M. (1992). *Mathematics and middle school students of Mexican descent: The effects of thematically integrated instruction.* (Research Report No. 5). Washington, DC: National Center for Research on Cultural Diversity and Second Language Learning, Center for Applied Linguistics.

Hooper, S., & Hannafin, M. J. (1988). *Cooperative learning at the computer: Ability-based strategies for implementation.* Paper presented at the annual meeting of the Association for Educational Communications and Technology, New Orleans, LA. (ERIC Document Reproduction Service No. ED295647)

Johnson, D. W., Johnson, R. T., Holubec, E. J., & Roy, P. (1984). *Circles of learning.* Alexandria, VA: Association for Supervision and Curriculum Development.

Klinger, J. K., & Vaughn, S. (2000). The helping behaviors of fifth graders while using collaborative strategic reading during ESL content classes. *TESOL Quarterly, 34*(1), 69–98.

LeTendre, G. K., Hofer, B. K., & Shimizu, H. (2003). What is tracking? Cultural expectations in the United States, Germany, and Japan. *American Educational Research Journal, 40*(1), 43–89.

Morris, D., & Nelson, L. (1992). Supported oral reading with low-achieving second graders. *Reading Research and Instruction, 32*(1), 49–63.

Palinscar, A. M., Brown, A. L., & Campione, J. C. (1989, March/April). *Structured dialogues among communities of first grade learners.* Paper presented at the annual meeting of the American Educational Research Association, San Francisco.

Repman, J. (1993). Collaborative, computer-based learning: Cognitive and affective outcomes. *Journal of Educational Computing Research, 9*(2), 149–163.

Singhanayok, C., & Hooper, S. (1998). The effects of cooperative learning and learner control on students' achievement, option selections, and attitudes. *Educational Technology Research and Development, 46*(2), 17–33.

Slavin, R. E. (1995). *Cooperative learning: Theory, research, and practice* (2nd ed.). Boston: Allyn & Bacon.

Webb, N. M., & Farivar, S. (1994). Promoting helping behavior in cooperative small groups in middle school mathematics. *American Educational Research Journal, 31*(2), 369–395.

Welch, M., Richards, G., Okada, T., Richards, J., & Prescott, S. (1995). A consultation and paraprofessional pull-in system of service delivery: A report on student outcomes and teacher satisfaction. *Remedial and Special Education, 16*(1), 16–28.

Yager, S., Johnson, D. W., & Johnson, R. T. (1985). Oral discussion, group-to-individual transfer, and achievement in cooperative learning groups. *Journal of Educational Psychology, 77*(1), 60–66.

Chapter 4

Tutoring

Mary's decision to choose a highly motivating series of books for her young tutee proved to be just what Sarah needed. Because the book was about a young 9-year-old girl, just like herself, Sarah avidly began reading the book with her tutor's help, sometimes listening only, sometimes echo reading, sometimes reading aloud to her tutor. The book was interesting to Sarah in a way that previous books were not. It captivated her attention and drew her into the story. Her tutor indicated that the tutoring sessions consisted primarily of reading and discussing books from the American Girl series. Since Sarah was enchanted with the book, she was motivated to read for pleasure for the first time in four years of school experience. She kept a personal reading log of her books read outside of tutoring time and surprisingly was excited about the prospect of adding books to her log. (Cobb, 1998, p. 57)

T his description of one tutoring session was written by Jeanne Cobb in her 1998 case study of several low-achieving 4th-grade students. It illustrates the potential for tutoring to challenge and motivate a student. In this case the tutor, Mary, finds herself in the process of gradually introducing her student, Sarah, to a series of books and, more important, to reading. We can imagine Sarah's needs being uncovered and addressed as we see the two move ahead seamlessly from the first carefully chosen book and through other texts. Sarah, excited about her newfound skills, is clearly an emerging reader.

In This Chapter

• What the research has to say about tutoring and at-risk student achievement

• Discussion about the use of volunteer and professional tutors

• Practitioner implications

Cobb's case study provides one example of a successful intervention, but the apparent effectiveness of this tutoring session is not an exception. This is just one of a number of studies that examine the nature and effectiveness of tutoring as an approach to raising the achievement of low-performing students, and most of these studies indicate at least a moderate potential for success.

The relevant research reviewed by Snow for McREL's 2002 research synthesis (Barley et al., 2002) ranges from the case studies of individual tutors such as that presented by Cobb to one large quantitative program evaluation that tracked the performance of more than a thousand students (see Johnson, 1987). All in all, 23 studies representing the tutoring of 2,034 students inform the results shared here. Five of the studies are rich descriptions of specific cases, while the others employ quasi-experimental designs in an effort to provide evidence of the success of tutoring programs.

The logistics of the tutor–tutee sessions are not clearly described in all of the available research. In most cases, however, the descriptions do reveal that one tutor was placed with one tutee for a period of time. It is assumed that this personal, intense interaction is at the root of the potential for success of tutoring interventions. Note that this chapter does not include studies that involve peer tutoring. Peer tutoring is a strategy that is much more easily used within a classroom, a fact that raises different issues for teachers who may decide to employ the approach. Therefore, the peer tutoring research is discussed separately in the following chapter.

Even though there are differences in the sizes, the specific goals, and even the research methodologies of the programs studied, some common themes do emerge. This set of identified themes reveals an evidence-based foundation upon which approaches to tutoring low-achieving students can be based.

Program Review

Reflection Question

Who could your school turn to as sources for tutors?

One striking characteristic of the tutoring programs described in the research is that the program administrators have found capable tutors in a variety of circles. In a Denver program described by Tomlin (1995), for example, African American middle school boys are paired with high school contemporaries in hopes of encouraging both academic and personal growth. In California, senior citizens are brought in to schools to supplement reading instruction for Palo Alto elementary students (see McCarthy, Newby, & Recht, 1995), while a program in Marin County employs certified teachers to address the needs of 1st-grade low-performers (see Mantzicopoulos, Morrison, Stone, & Setrakian, 1992). The tutors in other programs studied range from older children (Jenkins, Jewell, Leicester, Jenkins, & Troutner, 1991) to college students (Cobb, 2001) to adults (Knapp & Winsor, 1998). Clearly, programs are leaving no stone unturned in their search for capable tutors.

In fact, some of the successful pairings described in the research may challenge the traditional notion of adult-and-child tutoring sessions. For example, in one study teacher–researcher Virginia Zukowski (1997) describes a successful pairing of one 5th-grade student, Raymond, with a 3rd-grade underachiever named Ian. Although the two are close in age, the relationship is clearly one of tutor and tutee (as opposed to peer tutoring) because Raymond is clearly not expected to gain academically from their meetings. In the following passage, the author likens this unique tutoring relationship to a pair working together to climb a hill on a tandem bicycle:

> Raymond, older and obviously more skilled, took charge and "broke the wind" for the ever struggling, yet hard working, Ian. He made Ian's efforts amount to a great deal as he coached him through challenging science texts and edited his stories for spelling and punctuation. Raymond added just the right amount of help so that Ian could see quick results. This carried over into Ian's solo efforts. Ian's efforts were pulled along by Raymond's strength as if they were taking a ride on their own tandem bike. Success bred success. For example, Ian's story about a fishing trip began as a run-on sentence piece that was barely legible. It was a germ of an idea waiting to be told. Raymond added his knowledge of story elements and writing conventions. Together, they produced a final draft of which Ian was very proud. Raymond and Ian burst into the classroom having finally finished the story and announced their intentions to read it from the author's chair. That was a first for Ian. He settled into the cushion of the author's chair and his eyes scanned the audience for Raymond. Raymond gave the thumbs up and Ian proceeded to read his story. (p. 86)

Although Ian started the 3rd grade two years behind most of his peers, his relationship with Raymond apparently helped to close that gap. His teacher noticed improvements in his writing and, as described above, Ian was given the opportunity to experience success despite his academic struggles. We see that what Zukowski describes as her careful matchmaking in pairing these two students resulted in a successful relationship between a 3rd-grade student and his 5th-grade tutor.

In considering the described relationship between Ian and Raymond, it becomes clear that it is not hard to imagine others stepping into Raymond's successful tutoring role. The tutoring research is replete with examples of students, adult volunteers, teacher-tutors, and retirees who can share successes that would sound quite similar to those felt by Ian. We are left with the conclusion that the potential for success in tutoring is not strongly linked to any vast knowledge or life experience of the tutor. Instead, the research makes it clear that it is the careful attention of any tutor that can make the relationship successful.

Despite the vast differences between the programs studied due to the variety of tutors employed, it is important to note that the variety in the characteristics of these tutors (age, profession, education) is not the only source of programmatic variation. Some of the programs are long-standing efforts, running for years, while others are new programs undergoing initial evaluation. Some are described as running like well-oiled machines, while others are works in progress. And the research also reveals that, although most of the programs are successful in terms of their academic goals, some are not. The variety of tutoring programs represented by available research is as rich as the variety of students these programs serve.

Readers of these program studies will see that each of them is interesting in its own right, but the truth about tutoring as a potentially successful intervention lies in the broad comparisons that can be drawn based on the collective body of evidence.

Results

Comparisons among the research yield some interesting results. For example, successful programs reportedly produced academic gains that would raise all but our lowest performers into an average range.[1] This observation is consistent with a recent synthesis conducted by Elbaum, Vaughn, Hughes, and Moody (2000). The idea that the individual attention offered by tutors can encourage academic growth is probably more comforting than it is surprising. However, with this potential for success in mind, we must consider more closely what it is about these successful programs that makes them so and, conversely, what it is about unsuccessful programs that contributed to their lack of success. Here, then, is a set of characteristics common to the success of the tutoring programs studied.

---

[1] In several of the successful studies included here achievement gains were reported in terms of an effect size of 0.3 to 0.8. The effect size is the difference between the treatment and comparison groups expressed in standardized units, or number of standard deviations. An effect size of 0.3 or greater is considered large enough to have practical meaning.

Achievement Through Feedback

Research has identified a strong relationship between feedback and achievement. In his book *What Works in Schools: Translating Research into Action,* education researcher Robert Marzano (2003) provides a review of the relevant research. After considering the results of five research syntheses, he indicates that "academic achievement in classes where effective feedback is provided to students is considerably higher than the achievement in classes where it is not" (p. 37).

Marzano also presents two specific characteristics that he sees as necessary for improved student learning. He suggests that feedback must be timely and that it must be specific to the content at hand. Clearly, the goal should be to provide relevant feedback while avoiding the confusion that can result from the introduction of extraneous information.

Note that the call for frequent formative information can also support the advocates of remedial tutoring programs. Tutoring is remarkably efficient in these terms given that the activity provides a constant flow of formative information. The ability to take full advantage of this flow of information appears to be the only limiting factor in its effectiveness. Tutoring, by nature of the activity, encourages the tutor to provide both timely and content-specific feedback, thus possessing the two essential characteristics set forth by Marzano. In this light we begin to see that tutoring is ideally suited for attending to the needs of students, particularly those at risk of academic failure.

Among the most interesting results is one that does not emerge. The available research provides no convincing evidence that the age, profession, or education level of the tutors influences the effectiveness of the programs they serve. Success was experienced by a wide variety of tutors including student tutors and community volunteers of all ages, as well as by licensed teachers. It appears as though any tutor with appropriate skills and an interest in tutoring can meet the needs of a low-performing tutee.

Central to the practice of tutoring is that the interaction is characterized by thorough and frequent diagnostic and prescriptive exchanges between tutor and tutee. This rich cycle of feedback and tailored instruction illustrated in both of the passages in this chapter allows the tutor to attend closely to the academic needs of the learner. In successful programs this exchange is recognized and encouraged. For example, the tutors in several programs were led through pre- and post-session meetings where they worked to customize and reflect on the session interactions (see in particular, McCarthy et al., 1995; and Richardson, Abrams, Byer, & DeVaney, 2000). In fact, the strong potential for the diagnostic–prescriptive exchange is likely responsible for the success experienced by the programs described in the research. This is no surprise because, for some time, researchers have noted the relationship between performance feedback and classroom success for students (see sidebar).

Successful tutoring programs also have what can be called a "guiding purpose." Consider a guiding purpose to be a strong theoretical backing or at least some expressed purpose that will help guide tutors in their decision making. One California study (Mantzicopoulos et al.,1992) describes a program in which each tutoring session prescribed a series of methods driven by differing reading theories. Mantzicopoulos et al. report that the purposive aim of the tutoring program gave the effort needed support. In Tennessee an informal guiding purpose was adopted by a program that merely encouraged its teachers to rely on their understanding of instruction in word families, vowel patterns, and complex contrasts while tutoring 1st-grade readers (see Morris, Tyner, & Perney, 2000). Regardless of the nature of the guiding purpose, its presence appears to provide a needed support for what would otherwise be a more complex environment for tutors.

A review of the research also suggests that ongoing evaluation and improvements of tutoring sessions appear to be an important part of the success of the programs studied. In many cases the quality of the tutoring programs is described in these terms including descriptions of supervision of tutoring sessions, continuing feedback for tutors, and pre- and post-session tutor meetings that support instruction. A successful program in Georgia encouraged supervisors to work with tutors to continually adjust the reading level of books for their different tutees (see Knapp & Winsor, 1998), whereas the lack of success in a Washington State program was attributed in part to a lack of ongoing tutor training throughout the semester (see Jenkins et al., 1991).

The logistical quality of volunteer tutoring programs is also a concern. Some programs are characterized by logistics of impressive quality. One example is a program that provides its tutors with tote bags filled with classroom supplies—dry erase boards, tablets, pencils, markers, and manipulatives—along with the training needed to use the materials to enhance their lessons (see Cobb, 2001). But indications of poor logistical quality were also reported. For example, the success of one North Carolina program was hampered by the logistics of permission slips and communication with teachers in their effort to bring college-age tutors into a local high school to work with at-risk teens (see O'Sullivan, Puryear, & Oliver, 1994). The program was relatively unsuccessful.

The research also suggests that tutoring programs do not need to be attached to some large-scale intervention (a published reading curriculum, for example) in order to be effective. Although some of the programs described in the research were connected to these large-scale efforts, such a foundation did not guarantee success nor did it seem to be necessary for producing success. In fact, more than half of the programs studied were able to demonstrate success without the support of a large-scale program.

Sarah's tutoring session, described in the opening vignette, and Ian's successful time with his tutor Raymond illustrate much of the potential that is found in the evidence-based tutoring research. For Sarah and Ian, and for all of the nation's low-performing students, there are a number of implications that can be drawn from the tutoring research.

Implications

The research supplies strong evidence that . . .

> . . . tutoring is an effective strategy for addressing the needs of low-performing students.

The research also suggests that . . .

> . . . tutoring programs should have a strong guiding purpose in order to direct the program tutors in their decision making. This guiding purpose should emphasize the diagnostic and prescriptive interaction that is a natural product of tutoring.

> . . . individuals of various ages and levels of education can be effective tutors once provided with appropriate training.

> . . . given their individualized nature, tutoring sessions need to be evaluated on a continual basis to ensure the day-to-day integrity of the intervention.

> . . . logistical concerns such as availability of materials, instructional space, and session scheduling can have a significant effect on the success of a tutoring program. In keeping with this notion, finding quality tutors also should be a primary concern.

References

Barley, Z., Lauer, P. A., Arens, S. A., Apthorp, H. S., Englert, K. S., Snow, D., & Akiba, M. (2002). *Helping at-risk students meet standards: A synthesis of evidence-based classroom practices* (REL Deliverable #2002-20). Aurora, CO: Mid-continent Research for Education and Learning. Available online at www.mcrel.org

Cobb, J. B. (1998). The social contexts of tutoring: Mentoring the older at-risk student. *Reading Horizons, 39*(1), 49–75.

Cobb, J. B. (2001). The effects of an early intervention program with preservice teachers as tutors on the reading achievement of primary grade at risk children. *Reading Horizons, 41*(3), 155–173.

Elbaum, B., Vaughn, S., Hughes, M. T., & Moody, S. W. (2000). How effective are one-to-one tutoring programs in reading for elementary students at risk for reading failure? A meta-analysis of the intervention research. *Journal of Educational Psychology, 92*(4), 605–619.

Jenkins, J. R., Jewell, M., Leicester, N., Jenkins, L., & Troutner, N. M. (1991). Development of a school building model for educating students with handicaps and at-risk students in general education classrooms. *Journal of Learning Disabilities, 24*(5), 311–320.

Johnson, J. (1987). *Adaptation of curriculum, instructional methods, and materials component: Instructional aide program. Final evaluation report.* Columbus, OH: Columbus Public Schools.

Knapp, N. F., & Winsor, A. P. (1998). A reading apprenticeship for delayed primary readers. *Reading Research and Instruction, 38*(1), 13–29.

Mantzicopoulos, P., Morrison, D., Stone, E., & Setrakian, W. (1992). Use of the SEARCH/TEACH tutoring approach with middle-class students at risk for reading failure. *The Elementary School Journal, 92*(5), 573–586.

Marzano, R. J. (2003). *What works in schools: Translating research into action.* Alexandria, VA: Association for Supervision and Curriculum Development.

McCarthy, P., Newby, R. F., & Recht, D. R. (1995). Results of an early intervention program for first grade children at risk for reading disability. *Reading Research and Instruction, 34*(4), 273–294.

Morris, D., Tyner, B., & Perney, J. (2000). Early steps: Replicating the effects of a first-grade reading intervention program. *Journal of Educational Psychology, 92*(4), 681–693.

O'Sullivan, R. G., Puryear, P., & Oliver, D. (1994, April). *Evaluating the use of learning styles instruction to promote academic success among at-risk 9th graders.* Paper presented at the annual meeting of the American Educational Research Association, New Orleans, LA.

Richardson, G. D., Abrams, G. J., Byer, J. L., & DeVaney, T. W. (2000, November). *UWA secondary education tutoring project for the West Alabama Learning Coalition.* Paper presented at the annual meeting of the Mid-South Educational Research Association, Bowling Green, KY.

Tomlin, V. E. (1995). A mentor program for improving the academic attainment of Black adolescent males. *Dissertation Abstracts International, 55*(9-A), 2728. (UMI No. 9502892)

Zukowski, V. (1997). Teeter-totters and tandem bikes: A glimpse into the work of cross-age tutors. *Teaching and Change, 5*(1), 71–91.

Chapter 5

Peer
Tutoring

Jason and Tiffany were in a cozy area of the library corner, each holding a stuffed tiger. Although both children were assigned to basic skills classrooms, in the present situation Tiffany assumed the role of teacher to help Jason, who had started looking through a book of nursery rhymes.

"Let's read this one," Tiffany said. Jason agreed, and Tiffany told him to begin reading. "I forgot the first word. What does H-E-Y say?" "That says, 'Hey diddle diddle'" said Tiffany. "Now you read." Jason continued, "The cat and the . . ." He paused, and Tiffany said, "Look at the letter, it's an F. F. It says 'the fiddle.'" "Oh," said Jason, ". . . the fiddle. The cow jumped over the moon. Let's do another one." Tiffany said okay. They turned the page and Jason began to read: "Little Betty Blue lost her shoe." "Wait," Tiffany interrupted, "You gotta read the title first." (Morrow, Rand, & Young, 1997, p. 14)

T hese observations on the opposite page were reported by the authors as an example of social behavior in peer tutoring situations. They were surprised by Tiffany's interest in accepting the role of teacher as well as her ability to do so. Her confidence and patience are apparent. Jason's role is more passive, but he was the benefactor of a healthy dose of personalized instruction and he was willing to accept Tiffany's help. The reader gets the sense that both children are served in some small way by this encounter. Determining the extent to which peers can help each other to learn is the goal of this chapter.

Teachers often turn to alternate grouping strategies after their work with general instruction strategies has failed to meet the needs of their low-performing students. In an effort to promote alternate grouping strategies, Greenwood, Carta, and Hall (1988) cite inadequate evidence of effectiveness and methodological ambiguity in what they refer to as "teacher-mediated classroom procedures" (pp. 258–260). The potential benefits of the peer tutoring alternative, the authors contend, include the proven ability for these interventions to work effectively in a variety of contexts, and the natural social response of students, which appears to improve learning attitudes and classroom behavior.

A closer look at the 30 studies discussed in this chapter reveals a variety of programs that can inform practice. Many of these studies are large-scale, thorough analyses of established programs. The number of students who were exposed to a peer tutoring intervention in each study varied from just a few to hundreds (the average was 71 students). Each of the studies was designed in keeping with experimental models and reported quantitative results. Before the results reported by Barley (2000) for McREL's 2002 research synthesis are considered, however, a sense of the diversity in these programs will be provided.

In This Chapter

• What the research has to say about peer tutoring and at-risk student achievement

• CWPT (Classwide Peer Tutoring)

• PALS (Peer-Assisted Learning Strategies)

• RPT (Reciprocal Peer Tutoring)

• Practitioner implications

Program Review

In the opening passage, Jason and Tiffany were paired in a peer tutoring session. Jason quickly slipped into the role of the tutee as Tiffany became his tutor. Even in random pairings, a similar relationship is often the result: One student becomes the tutor and the other student steps into the role of the learner. This is dealt with in different ways in the studied programs, but a general description of peer tutoring interventions does emerge from the research. First, the teacher assigns students to pairings (either randomly or intentionally). She then clearly defines roles for both tutor and tutee, and a schedule is maintained that has the students switching roles.

A California study of second-language 1st graders is one example of a program that deals closely with this natural inclination for students to assume roles in peer pairings (Cardona & Artiles, 1998). The varying language skill levels in these classrooms result in an academic diversity that is not expected in groups of 1st-grade students. The program addresses this issue by intentionally pairing the low-achieving students with their higher-performing peers. These students, too, are asked to switch roles during each session, but the programmatic goal is clearly that of bringing the low performers closer to the ability level of their peers.

This California study is unique within the 30 included studies in that it is the only study that is not closely aligned with one of three programmatic strands. The remaining 29 studies examine programs that use one of these intervention strategies:

- Classwide Peer Tutoring (CWPT)
- Peer-Assisted Learning Strategies (PALS)
- Reciprocal Peer Tutoring (RPT)

Any search of recent peer tutoring research will return studies that in many cases refer to these three specific interventions. CWPT, PALS, and RPT were all conceived in university settings, each has clearly defined characteristics, and each has been implemented and studied repeatedly. Since each of the studies is quite similar to the others within that strand, the studies will be presented as a group under these three program headings.

Classwide Peer Tutoring

Classwide Peer Tutoring (CWPT) is a product of the Juniper Gardens Children's Project at the University of Kansas (Greenwood et al., 1987). This intervention is well defined and has been thoroughly studied (see, in particular, Greenwood, 1991; Greenwood, Delquadri, & Hall, 1999; and Greenwood, Arreaga-Mayer, Utley, Gavin, & Terry, 2001). In fact, 15 of these studies recorded effects on at-risk students and were, therefore, included in the body of work that informs this chapter.

The intervention itself requires a set of specific program characteristics.[1] CWPT students are chosen randomly to form peer tutoring pairs. In any given session each of the students in the pair serves as the tutor for 10 minutes, and then switches roles to become the tutee for 10 minutes. The programs studied allowed an extra 10 minutes for logistics, leaving them with 30-minute sessions that met between two and five times each week. The pairings were changed weekly, and careful records were maintained. As described, CWPT students work with basic skill acquisition (spelling, vocabulary, and basic math skills) while competing with other groups for points that correspond to academic growth. The programs studied generally reported positive results.

This description of one intervention presented by Madrid, Greenwood, Whaley, and Webber (1998) provides a better sense of what a CWPT classroom looks like:

> Each Monday the teacher introduced 10 new 2nd-grade-level spelling words to the students. She pronounced each word and the children were asked to echo each word aloud and in

[1] For more information, contact the Juniper Gardens Children's Project (http://www.jgcp.ku.edu) or refer to Carta, Dinwiddie, Kohler, Delquadri, and Greenwood (1984).

unison. . . . On each day thereafter, for the remainder of the week, the teacher began the spelling session by saying, "We are going to play a game with spelling words. The purpose of the game is to earn as many points for yourself and your team as you can." The purpose of the points was only to determine the game winner. The teacher randomly divided the class into two teams. Within each team, students were paired into dyads. The class was informed that each day they would work with their teammate as a pair.

The randomly selected tutor was the person who read the spelling words from the spelling list. The randomly selected tutee wrote the word while at the same time spelling the word out loud to the tutor. Correctly spelled words earned two points from the tutor. If the word was misspelled, the tutor was to correctly spell the word slowly. The tutee received one point for modeling the correct spelling and writing of the word three times in a row on the answer sheet. If one of the three practice trials was misspelled, the tutee did not receive any points. . . . At the end of the 15-minute tutoring session the tutor assumed the tutee role and the tutee assumed the tutor role for an additional 15 minutes. (pp. 238–239)

The most apparent characteristic of this CWPT intervention is that the students are strongly encouraged to be actively engaged. This is particularly important when CWPT is compared to more traditional methods of teaching spelling. In fact, spelling skills may be well suited for this intervention. A student tutor in this context is more likely to be effective given the nature of the skill as well as the simplicity of the instruction that needs to take place.

Peer-Assisted Learning Strategies

Researchers at Peabody College of Vanderbilt University have developed, implemented, and studied a different intervention that incorporates peer tutoring. Peer-Assisted Learning Strategies (PALS) is a systematic strategy of providing feedback for use by teachers and students in skill acquisition (see Fuchs, Fuchs, Phillips, Hamlett, & Karns, 1995). Eight studies of PALS reading and math interventions were included in the McREL synthesis (Barley et al., 2002). As was seen in most of the CWPT research, these studies all reported significant increases in achievement for their low-achieving students.

Weekly classwide assessments drive the PALS process. The scores from these tests are used to determine student pairings for peer tutoring and to encourage the development of student goals for the tutoring sessions. The tutoring sessions themselves are quite similar to the CWPT intervention described above. The difference appears to be that PALS students are in competition only with themselves. They use the weekly assessment feedback to set goals and to gauge their own progress. The PALS process also emphasizes a steady flow of praise and communication between the tutor pairs, and provides the student tutor with a rigid structure for instructing. This structure is slowly removed as the student tutor gains confidence in the process.

> **Reflection Question**
>
> What are the advantages of using classroom assessment data to enhance peer tutoring?

This description by Fuchs et al. (1995) provides an example of the initial structure that can be provided by a student tutor:

> During PALS, every student in the class was paired to work on a mathematics operations skill with which the tutee required assistance and on which the tutor could provide help. Pairings were based on the [weekly test] data. During PALS, students worked through 12 instances of the target problem type. The tutor modeled a series of questions that the tutee could use to guide himself or herself to the problem's solution. Each question required a verbal or written response by the tutee. Questions differed by problem type. Tutors responded every time the tutee wrote a digit. When the tutee was correct, the tutor circled the digit and praised the tutee; when the tutee was incorrect or expressed confusion, the tutor provided additional help. Consequently, although interactions were structured, tutors were required routinely to construct their own explanations and strategies to provide this additional help. (p. 611)

Fuchs et al. go on to describe the increasing levels of independence that are afforded to the tutees as they begin to demonstrate competence. At the conclusion of each of these sessions the students are given a three-problem test to assess progress. This half-hour process is facilitated twice weekly for two weeks before the tutoring pairs are reassigned.

New Research on Peer-Assisted Learning (PAL)

Researchers who have long been interested in the peer-assisted learning (PALS) intervention have recently completed a synthesis of this specific peer tutoring strategy. Rohrbeck, Ginsberg-Block, Fantuzzo, and Miller (2003) combined the results of 90 studies and found that PALS accounted for an approximate growth of 22 percentiles in the achievement of participating students.

The authors report that PALS is more effective with at-risk students. Although low scores are by nature easier to raise, these results are still encouraging given the difficulties in reaching these students. This research indicates that peer tutoring, and PALS specifically, may emerge as a more important strategy in meeting the needs of at-risk students.

And, despite a design that relies on relative expertise in its tutors, role switching also occurs in PALS. The authors note that each student is assured the chance of being a tutor for at least two weeks during any given six-week interval.

Reciprocal Peer Tutoring

A third intervention based on the idea of peer tutoring was developed by researchers at the University of Pennsylvania. Reciprocal Peer Tutoring (RPT) is an intervention designed to enhance students' independence as learners and their effectiveness in cooperating with peers (see Fantuzzo, King, & Heller, 1992). There are six studies included in this chapter in which RPT is used to encourage academic growth in low-performing students. All of the programs analyzed in these studies served 4th- or 5th-grade mathematics students, and in five of the six studies positive results were reported.

RPT students are encouraged to focus on their own learning and to provide support for their peer tutoring partner. Most of the emphasis in this intervention is placed on learner control of the session goals and rewards (see Fantuzzo, Davis, & Ginsburg, 1995). The peer tutors are in place as a source of support for their partner rather than as a source of instruction. So, in the RPT classroom, the teacher retains the instructional responsibility (see Ginsburg-Block & Fantuzzo, 1997).

The specific RPT intervention sessions vary in length, but average between two and three hours over any given week. It also appears as though pairing assignments are likely to be random, but that the frequent reassignments seen in CWPT are not undertaken in RPT. This intervention, like the others, is used successfully to attend to basic, remedial skills.

In the following example intervention, RPT is being applied in an elementary math lesson (Fantuzzo, Polite, & Grayson, 1990). Prior to the peer tutoring sessions, the student pairs have already met with a teacher who helped them to determine individual and team goals:

> Each day during treatment the dyad performed the following sequence of tasks in the classroom: First, prior to arithmetic drills they took out their weekly scorecards and reminded each other of their individual and team goals. After the 5-minute arithmetic drill they exchanged papers and corrected each other's papers as the teachers read the answers to the class. Next, they counted the number their partner got correct and wrote this number at the top of their drill sheet and on their scorecard. They then returned the papers, rechecked their partner's count, and recorded their score on their scorecard. Next, they independently computed the dyad's total and compared the total with the team goal written on the top of the scorecard to determine if their team had "won." If the total was at or above the goal, they checked the "Win" box on the scorecard and gave themselves a happy face. If it was below the goal, they checked the "Try Again" box and administered no sticker. (pp. 313–314)

The students who engaged in this activity will not be expected to be experts in the curriculum or even to teach one another. Their roles are to serve each other as a source of moral support and as a logistical aide (for instance, by grading papers and verifying scores). This is typical of RPT and quite different from the interventions defined by CWPT and PALS.

Results

With or without minor changes, these peer tutoring approaches can be used in a wide variety of classrooms. Diversity, for example, could be addressed by defining the task for the group and then providing the different dyads with material of varying ability levels. The research also demonstrates the use of similar peer tutoring interventions in a variety of curricular areas which supports broad applications of the approach.

There are, however, limits to the conclusions that can be drawn from the overwhelmingly positive results reported in the available research. The majority of this research is focused on basic skill instruction in primary and elementary grades. It appears as though the effectiveness of a student tutor might be dependent on simplicity of content and the instructional role that the tutor is asked to take. This may be true to a lesser degree in Reciprocal Peer Tutoring given the nature of the peer relationship, but the homogeneity of the RPT research contexts—all taking place in 4th- and 5th-grade math classrooms— makes a determination difficult.

Implications

The research supplies strong evidence that . . .

> . . . peer tutoring can be an effective means for meeting the needs of at-risk or low-performing students, particularly in basic skills.

The research suggests that . . .

> . . . students need to be carefully instructed in their peer tutoring roles, and that they need to be monitored closely, in order to encourage program effectiveness.

> . . . peer tutoring sessions need to be highly structured in order to be effective with at-risk students.

References

Barley, Z., Lauer, P. A., Arens, S. A., Apthorp, H. S., Englert, K. S., Snow, D., & Akiba, M. (2002). *Helping at-risk students meet standards: A synthesis of evidence-based classroom practices* (REL Deliverable #2002-20). Aurora, CO: Mid-continent Research for Education and Learning. Available online at www.mcrel.org

Cardona, C., & Artiles, A. J. (1998, April). *Adapting classwide instruction for student diversity in math.* Paper presented at the Annual Convention of the Council for Exceptional Children, Minneapolis.

Carta, J. J., Dinwiddie, G., Kohler, F., Delquadri, J., & Greenwood, C. R. (1984). *The Juniper Gardens classwide peer tutoring programs for spelling, reading, and math: Teacher's manual.* Kansas City, KS: Bureau of Child Research, University of Kansas.

Fantuzzo, J. W., Davis, G. Y., & Ginsburg, M. D. (1995). Effects of parent involvement in isolation or in combination with peer tutoring on student self-concept and mathematics achievement. *Journal of Educational Psychology, 87*(2), 272–281.

Fantuzzo, J. W., King, J. A., & Heller, L. R. (1992). Effects of reciprocal peer tutoring on mathematics and school adjustment: A component analysis. *Journal of Educational Psychology, 84*(3), 331–339.

Fantuzzo, J. W., Polite, K., & Grayson, N. (1990). An evaluation of reciprocal peer tutoring across elementary school settings. *Journal of School Psychology, 28*(4), 309–323.

Fuchs, L. S., Fuchs, D., Phillips, N. B., Hamlett, C. L., & Karns, K. (1995). Acquisition and transfer effects of classwide peer-assisted learning strategies in mathematics for students with varying learning histories. *School Psychology Review, 24*(4), 604–620.

Ginsburg-Block, M., & Fantuzzo, J. (1997). Reciprocal peer tutoring: An analysis of "teacher" and "student" interactions as a function of training and experience. *School Psychology Quarterly, 12*(2), 134–149.

Greenwood, C. R. (1991). Classwide peer tutoring: Longitudinal effects on the reading, language, and mathematics achievement of at-risk students. *Reading, Writing, and Learning Disabilities, 7*(2), 105–123.

Greenwood, C. R., Arreaga-Mayer, C., Utley, C. A., Gavin, K. M., & Terry, B. J. (2001). Classwide peer tutoring learning management system: Application with elementary-level English language learners. *Remedial and Special Education, 22*(1), 34–37.

Greenwood, C. R., Carta, J. J., & Hall, R. V. (1988). The use of peer tutoring strategies in class-room management and educational instruction. *School Psychology Review, 17*(2), 258–275.

Greenwood, C. R., Delquadri, J. C., & Hall, R. V. (1999). Longitudinal effects of classwide peer tutoring. *Journal of Educational Psychology, 81*(3), 371–383.

Greenwood, C. R., Dinwiddie, G., Bailey, V., Carta, J. J., Dorsey, D., Kohler, F. W., et al. (1987). Field replication of classwide peer tutoring. *Journal of Applied Behavior Analysis, 20*(2), 151–160.

Madrid, D., Terry, B., Greenwood, C., Whaley, M., & Webber, N. (1998). Active vs. passive peer tutoring: Teaching spelling to at-risk students. *Journal of Research and Development in Education, 31*(3), 236–244.

Morrow, L. M., Rand, M. K., & Young, J. (1997). *Differences between social and literacy behaviors of first, second, and third graders in social cooperative literacy settings.* Rutgers University and Jersey City State College, NJ. (ERIC Document Reproduction Service No. ED406667)

Rohrbeck, C. A., Ginsburg-Block, M. D., Fantuzzo, J. W., & Miller, T. R. (2003). Peer-assisted learning interventions with elementary school students: a meta-analytic review. *Journal of Educational Psychology, 95*(2), 240–257.

Chapter 6

Computer-Assisted
Instruction

Imagine working through a set of math problems on a computer. As you solve each one, you move on to another. Eventually, a message appears on the screen:

> YOU ARE SHOWING GREAT IMPROVEMENT!! If YOU continue
> to improve while doing the next few problems YOU will be able
> to pass the harder problems and find them easy to solve.
> (Brawly, 1984, p. 66)

T he computer message is found in a program designed to encourage improved performance in mathematics students. Brawly (1984) wrote the program and then tested it with 120 2nd-, 4th-, and 6th-grade students in the early 1980s. Although his program and this message may be dated by today's commercial software standards, reading the message provides a sense of what it is like for today's students to be taught by computers.

In This Chapter

• What the research has to say about computer-aided instruction and at-risk student achievement

• Anticipated effects in reading and math instruction

• Practitioner implications

How low-performing students are taught by computers, as well as what students learn from them, is the focus of this chapter on Computer-Assisted Instruction (CAI). The chapter begins with program descriptions that illustrate the variety of computer uses in classrooms. These descriptions are followed by a review of the results of the available research and the results of a meta-analysis conducted by Akiba (see Barley et al., 2002) using this research. The results demonstrate that CAI has been effective in meeting the needs of at-risk students in a number of different contexts, and the meta-analysis of the available research results in a specific amount of growth that can be expected in certain contexts.

It is important to recognize, however, that often the question is not *whether* teachers or schools should expose their students to computer-assisted instruction, but rather how students should spend their computer time. U.S. Department of Education (2002) statistics indicate that although less than 20 percent of 4th graders used computers once each week in 1982, 70 percent were doing so by 1996. It may be that the nation's low-performing students are in many cases those who do not have weekly access to computers, but research on the effectiveness of CAI strategies for learning may help to further increase the flow of computers into schools.

What these statistics do not tell us is how students have been using their computer time. Research on CAI provides a partial answer to this question. In most cases research studies cite the use of specific commercial software packages.[1] In each of these studies, it is the nature of the software that is expected to define the nature of the student activity. These activities range from word processing to skill practice to programming. Unfortunately, a reference to a particular software title is often the only intervention description given. The computer message at the start of this chapter is, therefore, a rare glimpse into the workings of a CAI classroom.

Seventeen studies are reviewed in this chapter on CAI. All of this research involves quasi-experimental designs including the use of pre- and post-testing and comparison groups. The number of at-risk students exposed to CAI in each of these studies ranges from 4 to 824, with an average of 101 at-risk students per study. A sense of what these students are doing as they learn through CAI sessions is provided in the following paragraphs as the programs, and their similarities and differences, are described.

Program Review

The program variety seen in the CAI research is the result of the variety found in the available instructional software. For example, a group of four 1st graders in the Southeast were exposed to two different CAI interventions (see Emihovich & Miller, 1988). Two of the students spent an hour each week working with LOGO[2] (a geometric programming language). The other two students spent the same amount of time working with software designed to tutor mathematics skills and concepts. Emihovich and Miller report that the LOGO students demonstrated greater achievement gains. This is an encouraging result in terms of the potential for open-ended programs such as LOGO to help improve the performance of minority math students.

---

[1] *There is a wide variety of software products available, too many to mention here. Because of the many possible choices, it may be difficult to find software that is suitable and has been tested in a classroom environment. Note that software publishers should be able to direct consumers to any relevant third-party research or reviews.*
[2] *LOGO is a user-friendly geometric software that makes it possible for students to begin programming at a very young age. See Papert (1980).*

In a California program studied by Moore (1988), 7th- and 8th-grade mathematics teachers used CAI extensively in their classes. Curricular weaknesses of 61 low-performing students were identified using paper-and-pencil tests, and then these problem areas were addressed by giving the students a computer-based assignment in one of two commercial software packages. During the computer sessions, the teachers circulated and served as tutors. The study found that all of the computer-assisted students showed significant gains encouraged by CAI, but that teachers with positive attitudes toward low-performing students had influenced the student gains to an even greater degree than had the CAI.

Reflection Question

Can computers tutor students? Are there limits to the effectiveness of CAI?

Other studies of CAI mathematics programs appear to be direct efforts to evaluate the effectiveness of specific software programs. Ninth-grade math students in Virginia, for example, engaged in CAI drill and practice, simulations, and games, in a program designed to increase ability (see Bailey, 1991). The 21 students involved in the CAI group were identified as low-performing based on their standardized test scores. Based on a comparison of pre- and post-tests, Bailey reports that these students increased their academic ability as a result of the computer-based instruction. In a North Carolina program, 60 7th- and 8th-grade low-performing students used a commercial CAI program for instruction and practice to support the middle school math curriculum (see Kestner, 1989). Again, Kestner reports a significant increase in the mathematics skills of these students.

A significant amount of CAI research also has been done in the fields of reading and writing instruction. In one such study (Adams, 1986), 45 middle school students in Mississippi engaged in computer-assisted reading instruction. For this group of inner-city students, the commercial software produced mixed results. The same was true in a Pennsylvania study of 20 middle school students (see Kochinski, 1986). These 6th- through 8th-grade students were below grade level in reading but did not seem to benefit from the commercial reading software. Wepner (1991) also reports mixed results from her study of 8th-grade students who used reading and writing software for

Groups Working with Computers

Computer-assisted instruction (CAI) also has been shown to have positive effects with small groups of students. In a synthesis of 122 studies, researchers Yiping Lou, Philip Abrami, and Sylvia d'Apollonia (2001) found that small groups of students learned more than students who worked alone during CAI sessions. The studies that these authors reviewed described a wide variety of CAI designs, as well as grouping strategies including cooperative learning, and they found that small-group CAI sessions of any sort were similarly effective in promoting achievement.

The authors do note that students working alone spent more of their time interacting with the computer and, therefore, were able to accomplish tasks faster. But the speed of the individual learners seems to have come at a price. The students in small groups learned more, relied more heavily on effective learning strategies, demonstrated more perseverance, and were less reliant on their teachers for help.

For more information on the effectiveness of small-grouping strategies, see the Small Groups chapter in this book.

40 minutes each week. These inner-city New Jersey students reportedly were engaged by stories involving relevant issues, but their interest did not translate into measurable achievement gains. Dellario (1987) reports the results of a study of three different commercial software packages that were used prescriptively in Michigan. In this study, however, most of the 95 low-performing 9th-grade students demonstrated academic growth at the conclusion of the intervention.

Two of the studies included in this section researched CAI effects on multiple subject areas on a large scale. The largest of these is a Massachusetts study of 824 2nd through 6th graders (see Sinkis, 1993). Sinkis reports academic growth for most of these Chapter I students in reading and in mathematics. Dungan (1990) reports mixed results in another large study, this one involving 121 Mississippi elementary students who were exposed to software designed to improve their skills in reading, language arts, writing, and math. Despite being taught and drilled in these subjects for an hour each week, the students failed to demonstrate significant growth in any of the subjects.

Results

The nature of the design of the studies included in this chapter, along with the way the results were reported, made it possible to conduct a meta-analysis of the available data. A meta-analysis is a quantitative synthesis of outcomes from a variety of smaller studies. Once combined in this systematic fashion, the size of an overall effect is determined. In terms of CAI research, this means that the available data were substantial enough to allow predictions about the amount of academic growth that should be expected as a result of using CAI in certain contexts.

As a part of her work, Akiba translated the academic growth of CAI students, as well as the academic growth of the students in the comparison groups, into percentile gains. The result is that an average student in CAI can be expected to score 14 percentile points higher than the average student involved in more traditional instruction as a result of careful intervention. It becomes clear that the issue raised earlier is particularly salient in light of the proven ability for CAI to assist low-achieving students. Namely, it is not *whether* students should be exposed to computers, but how their time on computers should be spent.

The answer to this question lies in the moderating factors identified by Akiba in her analysis (see Barley et al., 2002, p. 101). The most important moderating factor in determining the expected results of CAI is the subject area at hand. At-risk students learning mathematics, Akiba notes, are more likely to realize academic growth than those studying reading. Other identifiable factors, such as the grade level, the specific nature of the CAI activity (drill vs. project, for example), and the quality of the study itself, were not identified by the meta-analysis to have a significant effect on the results of the studies. Akiba does state, however, that reported differences in teacher facilitation activities and attitudes may have had an important influence on the results. A lack of careful description of the teacher's role in CAI sessions in most of the studies makes the significance of this teaching factor difficult to determine.

Implications

The research supplies strong evidence that . . .

   . . . computer-assisted instruction is an effective strategy for meeting the needs of at-risk and low-performing students.

The research suggests that . . .

   . . . computer-assisted instruction for at-risk students is more effective in mathematics than in reading or writing.

   . . . other factors, such as the grade level of the students and the design of the software being used, seem to have little effect on the resulting academic growth.

   . . . the role of the teacher in the computer-assisted intervention is significant.

References

Adams, C. R. (1986). Reading achievement of low socioeconomic seventh- and eighth-grade students with and without computer-assisted instruction. *Dissertation Abstracts International, 47*(11A), 3956.

Barley, Z., Lauer, P. A., Arens, S. A., Apthorp, H. S., Englert, K. S., Snow, D., & Akiba, M. (2002). *Helping at-risk students meet standards: A synthesis of evidence-based classroom practices* (REL Deliverable #2002-20). Aurora, CO: Mid-continent Research for Education and Learning. Available online at www.mcrel.org

Bailey, T. E. (1991). The effect of computer-assisted instruction in improving mathematics performance of low-achieving ninth-grade students (remediation). *Dissertation Abstracts International, 52*(11A), 3849.

Brawly, G. L. (1984). Effects of types of reinforcers and an achievement motivator interacting with aptitude on latency rate in computer-assisted mathematics instruction. *Dissertation Abstracts International, 46*(01A), 0058. (UMI No. 8504171). [*Note:* This study was not included in the McREL synthesis because it did not fall within the 1985–2002 time window.]

Dellario, T. E. (1987). The effects of computer-assisted instruction in basic skills courses on high-risk ninth-grade students. *Dissertation Abstracts International, 48*(04A), 0892.

Dungan, S. A. P. (1990). The relationship between computer-assisted instruction and the academic gains of selected elementary students in a rural school district. *Dissertation Abstracts International, 51*(10A), 3315.

Emihovich, C., & Miller, G. E. (1988). Effects of Logo and CAI on black first graders' achievement, reflectivity, and self-esteem. *Elementary School Journal, 88*(5), 473–487.

Kestner, M. K. (1989). A comparative study involving the administration of computer-managed instruction in a remedial mathematics program. *Dissertation Abstracts International, 51*(03A), 0774.

Kochinski, V. A. (1986). The effects of CAI for remediation on the self-concepts, attitudes, and reading achievement of middle school readers (Chapter 1, affective). *Dissertation Abstracts International, 47*(06A), 2100.

Lou, Y., Abrami, P. C., & d'Apollonia, S. (2001). Small group and individual learning with technology: A meta-analysis. *Review of Educational Research, 71*(3), 449–521.

Moore, B. M. (1988). Achievement in basic math skills for low-performing students: A study of teachers' affect and CAI. *Journal of Experimental Education, 57*(1), 38–44.

Papert, S. (1980). *Mindstorms: children, computers, and powerful ideas.* New York: Basic Books.

Sinkis, D. M. (1993). A comparison of Chapter One student achievement with and without computer-assisted instruction (Chapter One students, at risk). *Dissertation Abstracts International, 54*(2A), 0422.

U.S. Department of Education. (2002). *The facts about 21st century technology.* Retrieved from http://www.nclb.gov/start/facts/21centtech.html.

Wepner, S. B. (1991, October). *The effects of a computerized reading program on "at-risk" secondary students.* Paper presented at the annual meeting of the College Reading Association, Crystal City, VA.

Strategies to Assist Low-Achieving Students

Discussion
Guide

This section is designed to encourage discussion about effective teaching and at-risk students. The contents of this book are summarized on the following pages to inform discussion, and discussion questions are provided throughout the section to provoke conversation.

General Discussion Questions

Consider one or more of the strategies presented in this book. Use the following questions to guide discussion on the use of the strategy or strategies in your attempts to bring your low-performing students up to standards.

1. Have you tried the strategy? If so, what was your experience with it? If not, would you want to now?

2. Is the strategy best suited for math, reading, or some other subject area? Where could it be used most effectively in your curriculum?

3. Do the program examples provided in the strategy chapter seem similar to situations you have experienced in your classroom? What would make your students more or less likely to experience success with the strategy?

4. What are the most important factors in making the strategy effective? Would these factors make the use of the strategy difficult to facilitate in your classroom?

5. Could you imagine using all of these strategies in a school year? A week? A day? What would be the advantages and disadvantages of using a variety of strategies?

Key to Understanding Findings

Each of the six classroom strategy categories is summarized on the following pages. The summaries include a category description, an indication of the amount of available research used as a basis for claims, and an abbreviated set of findings. Each finding is presented under one of the following headings:

• *Evidenced*—The research supports a claim that observed gains in achievement can be attributed to a given intervention. Consistently large gains increase the confidence of these claims.

• *Promising*—The body of available research reveals a promising trend. These trends were identified by McREL as directions for further research. They are presented here for practitioner consideration.

• *Absent*—It is occasionally noteworthy to identify interventions that have not been shown to be effective.

Whole-Class Instruction

Description

The group of studies synthesized under this heading represents a set of whole-class interventions that support either a behaviorist or constructivist instructional approach.

Availability of Research

Fifteen studies were included in the whole-class research synthesis. Only four of these were coded by McREL as being high in quality. One of the high-quality studies researched a behaviorist intervention while three others researched programs that employed a constructivist approach.

Findings

It is important to note that several of the studies in this category were studies of a blended approach—infusing behaviorist approaches into a constructivist design or vice versa. There were studies that drew comparisons between approaches and those that merely made claims about the effectiveness of one approach. It is from this body of work that we draw the following conclusions.

Promising

In choosing between a behaviorist and constructivist approach, a practitioner should take the content into consideration. The available research indicates that a behaviorist approach is more likely to support a behavioral outcome while a constructed outcome is most effectively produced by a constructivist approach. For example, direct instruction in vocabulary was found to increase skills in vocabulary, but these learned skills did not generalize to other reading areas.

Absent

There is not enough evidence to determine whether one approach—behaviorist or constructivist—is superior to the other, nor does the evidence suggest that such a determination will emerge.

Additional Discussion Questions

1. The passage on page 14 describes a student coming to understanding of a book by relating it to his own experiences. Have you seen this in your classroom? If so, describe a similar situation. Are there subjects or topics that lend themselves to students frequently constructing their own understandings?

2. The passage on page 16 describes a curricular regimen utilized in a reading classroom. What are your experiences with interventions of this sort? What are the advantages and disadvantages of closely following a regimen like the one described?

Cognitively Oriented Instruction

Description

Cognitively oriented strategies have been defined by us as any approach that guides teachers in teaching students how best to learn. Such an approach is designed to help students improve the quality of their thinking and, therefore, support them in all curricular areas. This category includes analyses of both cognitive ("how-to" strategies and procedures) and metacognitive (planning, preparation, idea generation, as well as monitoring, self-checking, and revising strategies) instruction.

Availability of Research

Fifteen studies were included in the cognitively oriented strategies synthesis. Only five of these were coded by McREL as being high in quality.

Findings

The evidence reviewed in this chapter for the effectiveness of cognitively oriented instruction should encourage both the use of this approach for low-achieving students and further research of these cognitive interventions.

Promising

In reading instruction, a combination of instruction and practice in planning and preparation and summarizing strategies appears to be effective for low-achievers.

In writing and oral language, instruction in how to start, draft, and revise essays and speeches, combined with peer problem solving and feedback, appears to be effective.

In mathematics instruction, a combination of social contexts, peer modeling, meaningful problems to solve, and strategy instruction appears to be effective.

Additional Discussion Questions

1. The sidebar on page 24 describes reading instruction as a general metacognitive skill. Describe other, more specific cognitive or metacognitive skills that you teach in your classes. (For descriptions of these interventions beyond what is provided above, see the working definitions and examples of cognitive and metacognitive interventions provided on page 24.)

2. The implications in this chapter suggest that reading, writing, and mathematics instruction can be enhanced by cognitive and metacognitive instruction, but that teaching in the subjects should employ different sequences of approaches. Is it clear why this might be the case?

Small Groups

Description

The interventions addressed here are those that incorporated different strategies for dividing a classroom into smaller groups of students. The available research revealed heterogeneous and homogeneous grouping efforts including multiple subject area instruction, differentiation, and cooperative learning interventions.

Availability of Research

Eighteen studies were included in the small-group synthesis. Only five of these were coded by McREL as being high in quality.

Findings

The recent research suggests that some grouping strategies can have a positive impact on low-achieving students. These findings are encouraging given the increasing diversity faced by today's teachers.

Evidenced

Cooperative learning, when implemented in a rigorous manner, can provide students with enriched instruction through peer interaction. In the best cases, this interaction results in increased student achievement.

Appropriate training is integral to successful schoolwide implementation of cooperative learning strategies.

Absent

There is a lack of available research that would either support or condemn the use of homogeneous (ability) grouping. The research that shows positive results lacks the rigor we regard as necessary to present this approach as being one that shows promise.

Additional Discussion Questions

1. To what extent are small groups an effective part of your teaching? Describe a lesson that exemplifies the importance of small groups.

2. Does the passage on page 34 leave you the impression that it was effective? Guess how the teacher may have prompted the students before they began their conversation. What characteristics of small-group instruction do you feel are essential to its potential to be effective?

Tutoring

Description

Tutoring is defined as a one-on-one interaction between tutor and student. The tutors in the programs studied varied widely, from children to retirees, while in most cases the tutees were young readers. Studies of cross-age student tutoring interventions were included if it was clear that the tutor was not expected to gain academically from the tutoring interaction.

Availability of Research

Twenty-three studies were included in the tutoring synthesis. Only five of these were coded by McREL as being high in quality.

Findings

The recent tutoring research suggests that tutoring can be an effective approach in serving at-risk students. The studies of the tutoring synthesis are largely studies of early literacy, and it is from this body of work that we draw the following conclusions.

Evidenced

Tutors with virtually every level of education have been used effectively for early literacy education as long as the tutors were provided with appropriate training.

Evidence supports that diagnostic and prescriptive interactions are encouraged in effective tutoring practice.

Promising

Effective tutoring sessions are characteristically monitored and adapted with appropriate frequency.

A strong guiding purpose—a theoretical approach or step-by-step program structure—seems to be integral in an effective tutoring program.

Program logistics such as availability of materials, instructional space, and scheduling may have a significant effect on program results.

Finding, training, and retaining quality tutors should be a primary concern.

Additional Discussion Questions

1. This chapter suggests that tutoring is often limited by the availability of resources. Is lack of resources specifically limiting the amount of tutoring that occurs in your school? To what extent does your school take advantage of tutoring to help meet the needs of students who are below standards?

2. The passage on page 49 describes an older student tutor who appears to be having a positive effect on a younger at-risk student. Would this strategy help you to reach the low-achievers in your classroom?

Peer Tutoring

Description

Peer tutoring is defined as the individualized instruction of one student by another. In the available research a stronger student may have been paired with a weaker one or, in the case of students with even abilities, each student assumed the role of the tutor and the tutee during the instructional period.

Availability of Research

Thirty studies were included in the peer tutoring synthesis. Eleven of these were coded by McREL as being high in quality.

Findings

This research suggests that peer tutoring can be an effective approach for low-achieving students.

Promising

Preliminary evidence of the effectiveness of the following programs was found but limited to elementary-level students focused on basic skills:

• Classwide Peer Tutoring (CWPT)
• Peer-Assisted Learning Strategies (PALS)
• Reciprocal Peer Tutoring (RPT)

Absent

Research on peer tutoring interventions and their effects on middle and high school students is minimal and should be the focus of future research efforts.

Additional Discussion Questions

1. This chapter presents three specific approaches to peer tutoring. What are the differences between the approaches? To what extent might the strategies embedded in these approaches assist you in meeting the needs of your at-risk students?

2. Assessment data have an effect on the intervention described in the passage on page 61–62. What are the advantages of using assessment data in this manner? In what other ways do data affect your day-to-day practice?

Computer-Assisted Instruction

Description

Computer-assisted instruction is generally defined as an instructional process that uses a computer to present concepts or topics, monitor student growth, and adjust to needed advancements accordingly. The available research describes interventions that pair one or two students with each computer during sessions that involve relatively little teacher interaction.

Availability of Research

Seventeen studies were included in the computer-assisted instruction synthesis. Ten of these were coded by McREL as being high in quality.

Findings

The number and quality of the studies in this category made a meta-analysis possible. Based on this analysis and the resulting effect size (ES=0.37, or an approximate 14 percentile gain), we see that computer-assisted instruction can have a significantly positive effect on the achievement of at-risk students.

Evidenced

Computer-assisted instruction for at-risk students is more effective in mathematics than in literacy.

Promising

The training of the teacher-tutor and the resulting intervention may have a significant effect on the quality of a given computer-assisted instructional session.

Additional Discussion Questions

1. This chapter provides evidence that computer-aided instruction can and does have a significant effect on the achievement of at-risk students. Why do you suppose this intervention is so consistently effective? Why do you suppose that this intervention is more effective in math than in literacy?

2. Explore the notion that a computer can serve as a tutor for a student. In what ways can computers adopt the role of tutor, and in what aspects will the computers fall short?

A Final Note to Practitioners

A s a classroom professional, I am expected to allow research to guide my practice. This fact is made clear to me every time I read my district's professional standards or attend a school professional development session. I have attended to this expectation by absorbing what I can of the steady flow of research that comes my way. But, if you are like me, you may have noticed that the results of the research vary and sometimes even seem contradictory. For years I felt as though my efforts to be a research-based practitioner were pulling me in different directions. Eventually I began to cringe when my administrators began a sentence with the phrase "Research shows . . ." because it seemed to lead me more to frustration than to answers to questions I had about my teaching. What we need to realize (and what many have already come to realize) is that research is about many things and shows many things. There is an immense body of education research out there and, although it is meant to focus us, it can quite easily obscure our professional vision.

This book (along with the research synthesis on which it is based) has been an effort to compile strong, high-quality evidence that can be used to inform classroom practice. The results and implications provided in each chapter are in many cases limited in scope and lack the specifics that we all seek in our efforts to reach our at-risk students. Nonetheless, the results reported here are what good research shows about reaching these students. The unstudied practices and unreported specifics are not supported by evidence and, therefore, should not be accepted blindly.

In terms of my own practice, this lack of specific results carries with it a feeling of freedom. The results confirm some of my own notions about the effectiveness of tutoring and small groupings, and they have inspired me to explore peer tutoring and computer-assisted instruction. I no longer seek to maximize constructivist approaches in my classroom as I seek an effective balance between constructivist and behaviorist approaches instead. I have arrived at a new comfort within my practice and it is a comfort that has allowed me to consider new levels of instruction such as those suggested by the cognitively oriented program research. Most important, these results have freed me from frequent, abrupt changes in my instructional approaches and they have increased my confidence in being a research-based practitioner.

My hope is that you have found the information in this book to be of help to you in your practice.

My best to you in your important work,

David R. Snow

Index

ability grouping. *See* small-group instruction, like-ability
academic standards, state and local, 3
Akiba, M., 75
Apthorp, H. S., 23, 25
Arens, Sheila, 9–10, 12
at-risk, definition of, 5
audio tapes, for teaching reading, 16

balanced (constructivist-behaviorist) teaching strategies
    difficult to avoid, 18
    example of, 8, 10–12
    supported by research, 11, 82
behaviorism, 9–12
    definition of, 11–12
    knowledge, meaning of, 11–12
    opposed to constructivism, 10
behaviorist studies, no-nonsense language of, 15
behaviorist teaching strategies
    vs. constructivist, 12, 18–19, 82
    example of, 8, 11–12
    in math computation, 13
    quantifiable measures in, 17
    in reading, 15–17
    in spelling, 13, 19
    used for centuries, 11–12
Brawly, G. L., 70, 71

CAI. *See* Computer-Assisted Instruction
Circles of Learning, 41
classroom management, 10
class size, in public schools, 9
Classwide Peer Tutoring (CWPT), 60, 61–62. *See also* peer tutoring
    example of, 61–62
    random pairing in, 61
    in spelling, 61–62
coaches
    students as, in peer tutoring, example of, 58, 60
    teachers as
        in small-group instruction, 37, 41
        in writing, 30
Cobb, Jeanne, 47

coding the text, in reading, 26
cognitively-oriented instruction
 cognitive strategies
  definition of, 23–24, 84
  in different settings, 25
  "how-to" approaches, 24, 28, 84
  vs. metacognitive, 24–25
  in reading, 31
  step-by-step approaches, 24
  in writing, 28–29
 content-specificity of, 25–26
 definition of, 4, 84
 in mathematics, 29, 30–31, 84
  example of, 22
  paucity of studies on, 29, 30–31
 metacognitive strategies
  vs. cognitive, 24–25
  creativity and, 28
  definition of, 23–24, 84
  goal of, 24
  in mathematics, 31
  planning and preparation in, 24
  in reading, 31
  self-checking and revision in, 24
  in writing, 28–29
 in reading, 26–27, 84
 subject-area differences in, 25–26
 in writing, 27–29, 84
  paucity of studies on, 27
"collaborative strategic reading," 35
Computer-Assisted Instruction (CAI)
 grade-level and, 76
 in mathematics, 72–73, 92
  mixed results of, 74
 in mathematics *vs.* literacy, 76, 92
 in reading and writing, 73–74
  mixed results of, 73–74
 role of teacher in, 73, 76
computers
 increased availability of, 71
 small-group instruction and, 37–38, 74

       in teaching of different subjects, 37–38

       variety of classroom uses, 71

constructivism, 9–12

       definition of, 10–11

       knowledge, meaning of, 10–11

       opposed to behaviorism, 10

constructivist teaching strategies

       vs. behaviorist, 12, 18–19, 82

       in creative writing, 13

       example of, 8, 10–11

       in reading, 13, 19

cooperative learning, 4, 35–36, 86. *See also* small-group instruction

Cooperative Learning: Theory, Research, and Practice, 41

creativity, and metacognitive planning, 28

critical thinking, 23

CWPT. *See* Classwide Peer Tutoring

Department of Education, U.S., v, 71

diagnostic-prescriptive exchange, in tutoring, 51–52, 88

diversity, and peer tutoring, 66

evaluation and improvement, of tutoring programs, 52, 54, 88

evidence, strong, definition of, 6

evidence-based teaching strategies, need for, 3

evidenced, definition of, 81

exchange, diagnostic-prescriptive, in tutoring, 51–52

experimental studies

       definition of, 5

       paucity of, 5

feedback

       and achievement, 51

       peer, and writing, 28, 30

       and Peer-Assisted Learning Strategies (PALS), 62

       timeliness and specificity of, 51

flash cards, and mathematics, 15

grade-level, and Computer-Assisted Instruction (CAI), 76

Great Phonics Debate, 11

group, treatment, definition of, 5

grouping. *See* small-group instruction

Helping At-Risk Students Meet Standards: A Synthesis of Evidence-Based Classroom Practices, v

Institute of Educational Sciences, U. S. Department of Education, *v*
instruction. *See also* teaching strategies
    whole-class, 82
        definition of, 4, 19
        and traditional education, 4, 9
    whole language
        and constructivism, 11
        vs. phonics, 11

journals, and writing proficiency, 13
Juniper Gardens Children's Project, 61

knowledge
    behaviorist understanding of, 11–12
    constructivist understanding of, 10–11

learning how to learn, 4
library membership, encouraging, 15
literacy
    computers and, 76, 92
    vs. reading, 24
LOGO (geometric software), 72
low-performing, definition of, 5

mapping the text, in reading, 26
Marseglia, P., 13, 15–17
Marzano, Robert, 51
mathematics
    behaviorist whole-class instruction in, 13
    cognitively oriented instruction in, 29, 30–31, 84
        example of, 22
        paucity of studies on, 29, 30–31
    Computer-Assisted Instruction (CAI) in, 72–73, 92
        mixed results of, 74
    computers and, 37–38, 72–73, 92
    flash cards and, 15
    LOGO (geometric software), 72
    metacognitive teaching strategies and, 31
    pattern-recognition, in problem-solving, 29

Peer-Assisted Learning Strategies (PALS) in, 62–63
Reciprocal Peer Tutoring (RPT) in, 64–65
small-group instruction in, 37–38, 39–40
McREL (Mid-continent Research for Education and Learning), *v*, 3, 4, 9, 23, 35, 47,
    59, 62, 81, 82, 84, 86, 88, 90, 92
meta-analysis, definition of, 75
metacognitive strategies. *See* cognitively-oriented instruction
Moondance (short story), 13, 15–17, 18

National Council of Teachers of English, 11
National Reading Panel, 11
No Child Left Behind Act, 3

pairs
        highest and lowest paired
                in peer tutoring, 60
                in reading class, 16
        randomly assigned
                in Classwide Peer Tutoring (CWPT), 61
                in Reciprocal Peer Tutoring (RPT), 65
PALS. *See* Peer-Assisted Learning Strategies
paraprofessionals, in mixed-ability group instruction, 39
pattern-recognition, in solving math problems, 29
Peer-Assisted Learning Strategies (PALS), 60, 62–64. *See also* peer tutoring
        example of, 63
        and feedback, 62
        and mathematics, 62–63
        and reading, 62
        student roles in, 64
peer feedback, and writing, 28, 30
peer tutoring
        Classwide Peer Tutoring (CWPT), 60, 61–62
                example of, 61–62
                random pairing in, 61
                in spelling, 61–62
        definition of, 90
        diversity and, 66
        in higher grade levels, paucity of research on, 66, 90
        hybrid of small-group instruction and tutoring, 4
        monitoring needed for, 66
        Peer-Assisted Learning Strategies (PALS), 60, 62–64

example of, 63
in reading, example of, 58
Reciprocal Peer Tutoring (RPT), 60, 64–65
differences from CWPT and PALS, 65
example of, 65
learner control of goals and rewards in, 64
in mathematics, 64–65
random pairing in, 65
social behavior in, 59
structure needed for, 66
student roles in, 58–60
vs. teacher-mediated classroom procedures, 59
vs. tutoring, 47–49
types of (CWPT, PALS, RPT), 60
phonics
and behaviorism, 11, 15
vs. whole-language instruction, 11
project-based content, 29
promising studies, definition of, 81

quasi-experimental studies, definition of, 5

random assignment, in experimental studies, 5
reading
active interpretation in, 14
anticipation in, 14
audio tapes and, 16
behaviorist whole-class instruction in, 15–17
coding the text, 26
cognitively oriented instruction in, 26–27, 84
"collaborative strategic reading," 35
Computer-Assisted Instruction (CAI) in, 73–74
mixed results of, 73–74
constructivist whole-class instruction in, 13, 19
vs. literacy, 24
mapping the text, 26
as metacognitive skill, 24
pairing highest and lowest performers, 16
Peer-Assisted Learning Strategies (PALS) in, 62
peer tutoring in, example of, 58
phonics *vs.* whole-language instruction, 11

previewing the text, 26, 27, 30
Reciprocal Peer Tutoring (RPT) in, random pairing in, 65
and rereading, 15–17
small-group instruction in, 39–40
step-by-step approach to, 15–17
summarizing the text, 26, 27, 30
theater and reading proficiency, 13
tutoring in, example of, 46
use of student's personal experience in, 13–15
"REAP" (Read, Encode, Annotate, Ponder) program, 27
Reciprocal Peer Tutoring (RPT), 60, 64–65. *See also* peer tutoring
differences from CWPT and PALS, 65
example of, 65
learner control of goals and rewards in, 64
in mathematics, 64–65
random pairing in, 65
remedial tutoring, 51
roles, student
organizational, 35
in peer tutoring, 60
in Peer-Assisted Learning Strategies (PALS), 64
in small-group instruction, 35–36, 37
rote learning, 10
RPT. *See* Reciprocal Peer Tutoring

science
computers and, 38
small-group instruction in, 38
small-group instruction
computer use in, 37–38, 74
and cooperative learning, 4, 35–36, 86
heterogeneous (*see* mixed-ability *below*)
homogeneous (*see* like-ability *below*)
implications of method chosen, 37
interaction in, 37
like-ability (homogeneous), 36, 38–40
definition of, 36
expectations for, 42
less thoroughly studied than mixed-ability, 42, 86
not always planned, 38–39
in mathematics, 37–38, 39–40

mixed-ability (heterogeneous), 36, 37–38
    definition of, 36
    difficulties of, 39
    example of, 34
    not always an option, 38–39, 40–41
    paraprofessionals in, 39
    roles assigned in, 35–36, 37
    staff and preparation for, 41, 42
    vagueness of research on, 39
planning and, 41
in reading, 39–40
resources for, 40–41
roles in, differentiation of, 37
in social studies, 38
students as teachers in, 41
tasks in, clearly-defined, 37
teachers as coaches in, 37, 41
tracking and, 40
wide variety of, 35
in writing, 39
social studies
    computers and, 38
    small-group instruction in, 38
spelling
    behaviorist whole-class instruction in, 13, 19
    Classwide Peer Tutoring (CWPT) in, 61–62
standards, academic, state and local, 3
strategies. *See* cognitively-oriented instruction; teaching strategies
"strong evidence," definition of, 6
students
    at-risk, definition of, 5
    as coaches, in peer tutoring, example of, 58, 60
    low-performing, definition of, 5
    as non-teachers, in Reciprocal Peer Tutoring (RPT), 65
    second-language, 60
    as teachers
        in peer tutoring, 58, 59
        in small-group instruction, 41
    as tutees, in peer tutoring, 58, 60
    as tutors, in peer tutoring, 58, 60
Students Achieving Independent Learning (SAIL), 13–14

studies
    behaviorist, no-nonsense language of, 15
    experimental
        definition of, 5
        paucity of, 5
    meta-analysis of, 75, 92
        definition of, 75
    quasi-experimental, definition of, 5
    teacher's perspective on, 3

teachers
    as coaches, in small-group instruction, 37, 41
    role of, in Computer-Assisted Instruction, 73, 76
    as tutors, 48
teaching strategies. *See also* cognitively-oriented instruction
    balanced (constructivist-behaviorist)
        difficult to avoid, 18
        example of, 8, 10–12
        supported by research, 11, 82
    behaviorist
        vs. constructivist, 12, 18–19, 82
        example of, 8, 11–12
        in math computation, 13
        quantifiable measures in, 17
        in reading, 15–17
        in spelling, 13, 19
        used for centuries, 11–12
    blended (*see* balanced *above*)
    cognitive
        definition of, 23–24, 84
        in different settings, 25
        "how-to" approaches, 24, 28, 84
        vs. metacognitive, 24–25
        in reading, 31
        step-by-step approaches, 24
        in writing, 28–29
    constructivist
        vs. behaviorist, 12, 18–19, 82
        in creative writing, 13
        example of, 8, 10–11
        in reading, 13, 19

           student's personal experience in, 13–15

   evidence-based, need for, 3

   metacognitive

           vs. cognitive, 24–25

           creativity and, 28

           definition of, 23–24, 84

           goal of, 24

           in mathematics, 31

           planning and preparation in, 24

           in reading, 31

           self-checking and revision in, 24

           in writing, 28–29

terminology, 5

theater, and reading proficiency, 13

Title I students, 15

tracking, 40. *See also* small-group instruction

traditional education, 4, 9

treatment group, definition of, 5

tutoring. *See also* peer tutoring

   diagnostic-prescriptive exchange in, 51–52

   evaluation and improvement of, 52, 54, 88

   examples of, 46–47, 48–49

   guiding purpose for, 52, 54, 88

   and large-scale programs, 53

   logistical questions in, 53, 54, 88

   one-on-one, 47

   vs. peer tutoring, 47–49

   in reading, example of, 46

   remedial, 51

   variety of programs for, 50

   in writing, 48–49

           example of, 49

tutors

   age and education of, 51, 54, 88

   certified teachers as, 48

   children as, 48–49

   college students as, 48

   pre- and post-session meetings for, 52

   senior citizens as, 48

   sources of, wide range of, 4, 48–50, 88

   teachers as, in Computer-Assisted Instruction, 73

Weaver, Constance, 11
What Works in Schools: Translating Research into Action, 51
whole-class instruction, 82
    definition of, 4, 19
    in mathematics, 13
    and traditional education, 4, 9
whole language instruction
    and constructivism, 11
    vs. phonics, 11
writing
    cognitively oriented instruction in, 27–29, 84
        paucity of studies on, 27
    Computer-Assisted Instruction (CAI) in, 73–74
        mixed results of, 73–74
    constructivist whole-class instruction in, 13
    journals and proficiency in, 13
    of opinion essays, 28
    and peer feedback, 28, 30
    and revision, 28
    small-group instruction in, 39
    teachers as coaches, 30
    tutoring in, 48–49
        example of, 49

Zukowski, Virginia, 48–49

About the Authors

David R. Snow is a research consultant for Mid-continent Research for Education and Learning (McREL) and has served as an author on several large synthesis projects over the past several years. Qualitative analyses of research and writing for practitioner audiences constitute the bulk of his current work. His work for McREL is a natural extension of the qualitative evaluations he conducted while working for the Center for Instructional Research and Curriculum Evaluation (CIRCE) at the University of Illinois.

His 15 years of teaching experience range from serving as an instructor for Voyageur Outward Bound School in Minnesota to teaching at-risk students in the Chicago Public Schools. Much of his early interest in teaching and learning can be traced to his work as a program director for the American Youth Foundation and to his work as a volunteer for the YMCA. Snow currently lives in Denver and is a mathematics teacher at Grandview High School in Aurora, Colorado.

Snow received a bachelor of arts in mathematics education from the University of Toledo, a master of science in biomechanics from Michigan State University, and a master of arts in education from the University of Chicago, and is currently completing his doctoral work in curriculum and instruction at the University of Illinois. Recent emphasis in his work and studies has been placed on effective teaching practice guided by an explicit educational philosophy.

All correspondence should be directed to McREL, 2550 S. Parker Rd., Suite 500, Aurora, CO 80014. Phone: 303-632-5626. E-mail: dsnow@mcrel.org.

Zoe A. Barley has more than 15 years of experience in evaluating education programs. Barley joined Mid-continent Research for Education and Learning (McREL) in 1999 as Director of Evaluation, and soon assumed the position of Vice President for Research and Evaluation. In this position, she directs all research and evaluation work related to the Regional Educational Laboratory contract and the larger McREL organization, as well as independent evaluation contracts with other organizations and agencies. Prior to joining McREL, Barley was Director of Science and Mathematics Program Improvement (SAMPI) at Western Michigan University, Kalamazoo, Michigan, for 10 years. Under Barley's direction, SAMPI conducted the evaluations of Michigan's and Vermont's National Science Foundation-funded statewide systemic initiatives, Detroit's Annenberg Challenge Grant, the Michigan Mathematics and Science Centers Network, the Newaygo County Advanced Technology grant, W.K. Kellogg Foundation's science education program and Galileo Leadership initiative, and many others.

Barley pioneered in the development of cluster evaluation, a means of strengthening program implementation through formative evaluation while evaluating the impact of a group of similar projects. She has expertise in a wide range of evaluation and research methods and experience in applying them in local, state, and national contexts. Barley's work has included evaluating programs designed to improve student outcomes in low-performing schools. She also has studied programs designed to improve outcomes for girls and minority students, especially in mathematics and science.

Barley received a bachelor of arts from Harvard University, and a master of arts and doctorate in education from the University of Colorado.

Patricia A. Lauer is a principal researcher at Mid-continent Research for Education and Learning (McREL) in Aurora, Colorado. She is responsible for conducting, analyzing, and reporting on research related to teacher quality and school improvement, and she has written numerous technical reports for this work. Her research includes studies of award-winning teacher preparation programs, university–school partnerships, teacher learning in high-performing, high-needs schools, and online professional development for rural teachers. She led a team of researchers in writing case studies of collaborative action research partnerships with school districts, which resulted in a chapter for *Effective Educational Partnerships* (Praeger). She is also the lead author of a research synthesis on the effectiveness of out-of-school-time strategies in assisting low-achieving students in reading and mathematics. She recently authored an online research primer designed to help policymakers understand, evaluate, and use education research. She has given presentations on her work at ASCD and other conferences and has conducted workshops and trainings for school districts and universities.

Lauer received a bachelor of arts in psychology from the University of Nebraska at Omaha, and a master of arts and doctorate in experimental psychology from the University of Colorado at Boulder. Prior to joining McREL, she taught psychology and research methods at the college level for 15 years.

Lauer may be contacted at McREL, 2550 S. Parker Rd., Suite 500, Aurora, CO 80014. Phone: 303-632-5593. Fax: 303-337-3005. E-mail: plauer@mcrel.org.

Sheila A. Arens is an evaluator at Mid-continent Research for Education and Learning (McREL) in Aurora, Colorado. She has more than nine years of basic and applied research experience working in a variety of settings, including applied research and evaluation for nonprofit foundations and government agencies (e.g., correctional departments, judicial systems) as well as market assessments and evaluations for private industries and foundations. In addition, Arens has experience conducting analyses of education policies, notably those related to teacher education and induction; standards for preservice and in-service teachers; and various provisions of the No Child Left Behind Act of 2001.

Arens received a bachelor of arts in psychology and a master of arts in experimental psychology from the University of Colorado in Colorado Springs. She is currently completing her doctorate in inquiry methodology (with an emphasis in program evaluation) at Indiana University, Bloomington. In addition to working as an independent evaluation consultant, she has taught graduate-level courses in research methods and program evaluation at Indiana University, Bloomington, and has published in the areas of teacher education and program evaluation.

Arens may be contacted at McREL, 2550 S. Parker Rd., Suite 500, Aurora, CO 80014. Phone: 303-632-5265. Fax: 303-337-3005. E-mail: sarens@mcrel.org.

Helen S. Apthorp is a senior researcher at Mid-continent Research for Education and Learning (McREL). She is primarily responsible for building and continuing lines of research in the area of curriculum, learning, and instruction in collaboration with K–12 practitioners in McREL's seven-state regional educational laboratory service region. This position involves, but is not limited to, conducting literature reviews and field-based research, both quantitative and qualitative data analysis, and report writing. She serves as lead researcher on a study of high-performing, high-needs schools and continues to help lead McREL's research on the long- and short-term benefits of different models of school reform on teacher and student learning. Her current work in this area looks at effective instructional practices for diverse learners. Prior to joining McREL, she was a visiting assistant professor, Department of Educational Psychology, at the University of Connecticut, and an assistant professor of special education, Central Connecticut State University. She has been either conducting research and evaluation or teaching for the past 20 years.

Apthorp's expertise lies in the study of program effectiveness; the development of partnerships for professional learning; and the study of development, individual differences, and diversity. Specialties within these areas include reading development and disorders, learning disabilities, teaching groups of diverse students, instructional interventions to support literacy development of students with learning disabilities and other developmental disorders, literacy-oriented comprehensive school models, and the implementation of comprehensive school reform. Her special skills as they relate to this task order include research design, instrument development, quantitative and qualitative data collection and analysis, meta-analysis, graphic presentations of findings, project management, field-based research in school settings, and report writing.

Apthorp received a bachelor of arts in cognitive development from Hampshire College, a master of arts in educational psychology from the University of Colorado, and a doctorate in special education from the University of Connecticut.

Apthorp may be contacted at McREL, 2550 S. Parker Rd., Suite 500, Aurora, CO 80014. Phone: 303-632-5622. Fax: 303-337-3005. E-mail: hapthorp@mcrel.org.

Kerry S. Englert is a senior evaluator at Mid-continent Research for Education and Learning (McREL) in Aurora, Colorado. She has worked for more than eight years in applied educational research and psychometrics. Englert's research and publishing expertise lies in the areas of statistical analysis of data, assisting educators in using data from large-scale assessments and classroom assessments, and psychometrics. Specialties within these areas include mathematics professional development; international comparisons; gender differences in mathematics and science; and geography education.

Englert received a bachelor of science in engineering from Rochester Institute of Technology; a master of arts in communications from the University of Denver; a master of arts in measurement, evaluation, and statistical analysis from the University of Chicago; and a doctorate in education (with an emphasis in psychometrics) from the University of Colorado, Boulder. In addition to her experience as an evaluator and researcher, she has worked for the Colorado Department of Education as a psychometrician and was involved in all aspects of test development, administration, reporting of results, evaluating the psychometric properties, and conducting statistical analyses for the statewide testing program.

Englert may be contacted at McREL, 2550 S. Parker Rd., Suite 500, Aurora, CO 80014. Phone: 303-632-5627. Fax: 303-337-3005. E-mail: kenglert@mcrel.org.

Motoko Akiba is an assistant professor of educational policy studies in the Department of Educational Leadership and Policy Analysis at the University of Missouri-Columbia. Her expertise is school violence, multicultural education, and school reforms. Her work has been published in major education journals, including *American Educational Research Journal, Educational Evaluation and Policy Analysis,* and *Educational Researcher.* She has received numerous research grants to conduct quantitative policy analysis to investigate effective school conditions that promote student learning and health in the United States and other countries.

Akiba applies advanced quantitative methods such Hierarchical Linear Modeling (HLM), Structural Equation Modeling (SEM), and meta-analysis. She has received fully funded training from the National Center for Education Statistics (NCES) to conduct secondary analyses of large national and international databases such as NAEP, NELS:88, TIMSS, and PISA.

Akiba received a bachelor of arts in education from the University of Tsukuba, Japan, and dual-title doctorates in educational policy and comparative and international education from Pennsylvania State University–University Park. Prior to joining the University of Missouri–Columbia, she was a senior researcher at Mid-continent Research for Education and Learning (McREL) in Aurora, Colorado.

Akiba may be contacted at the Department of Educational Leadership and Policy Analysis, University of Missouri–Columbia, 202 Hill Hall, Columbia, MO 65211. Phone: 573-884-3730. E-mail: akibam@missouri.edu.